Akus & Bimbo

African Immigrants
Living A Godly Life

by

Felicia Oguntomilade

1663 Liberty Drive, Suite 200
Bloomington, Indiana 47403
(800) 839-8640
www.authorhouse.com

© 2004 Felicia Oguntomilade
All Rights Reserved.

No part of this book may be reproduced, stored in a retrieval system, or transmitted by any means without the written permission of the author.

First published by AuthorHouse 10/22/04

ISBN: 1-4184-6331-0 (e)
ISBN: 1-4184-6332-9 (sc)

Library of Congress Control Number: 2004094313

Printed in the United States of America
Bloomington, Indiana

This book is printed on acid-free paper.

DEDICATION

To all Africans, young and old, in diaspora.

To God who has the whole world in His Hand; the God who is the source and sustainer of His creations; the God who is all wise, all powerful, ever present and loving.

To Him be the glory forever.

ABOUT THE AUTHOR

Born at Ile -Ife Nigeria on June 16th 1933 into a christian family. Her parents, Mr. Emmanuel Ajayi and Mrs. Abigail Ibitayo Ajayi, were from Ado Ekiti, Nigeria. Felicia Ajayi attended the Queen's College both in Lagos and at Ede on full scholarship, and later trained as a nurse and midwife at the Teaching hospitals both in Nigeria and in England.

She got married in Manchester, England to Mr Jacob Oguntomilade an engineer student at Salford University, Salford, Lancashire, England; and since then they have been blessed with five grown up children, and also six grandchildren hitherto spread out into three continents: Africa, Europe and America.

Mrs Felicia Oguntomilade is a retired Chief Nursing officer and a Pastor's wife; she joined the husband in the Seminary at their middle age and they were both ordained Ministers of God.

She had traveled far and wide into Africa, Europe, and on Holy pilgrimage to the Holyland in the Middle East; and she now resides in the United States of America with her husband, a Professor of Theology at the National Bible College and Seminary at Fort Washington, Maryland.

Mrs Oguntomilade enjoys advising on Christian Counseling and also in giving needed care to her grandchildren and additionally actively supporting her husband in his Teaching Ministry.

She is gifted with mature understanding, wisdom, patience and good education having successfully earned the Doctorate degree in Theology (Th.D.) and honored with the Fellowship of the Faith Theological Seminary, Lagos.

                Prof. Jacob Oguntomilade,
                      (Husband)

ACKNOWLEDGMENTS

This book confirms the Word of God, which says" I can do all things through Christ that strengthens me". My absolute gratitude goes to my God who gave me the inspiration for this work. To him be the glory forever.

Since I stopped paid employment, my children have wondered how their mother will cope with all the free time available to her, as I have always been associated with lots of activities. I talked about the possibility of writing and since then, they have all encouraged me and believed I could do it with my wealth of experience. Thank you Kike, Bola, Peju, Dele, and Oye. You are very inspiring. As a token of my appreciation, my first book, "The Pilgrimage" which was about me, was printed and shared within the family. A special 'Thank You' goes to my latest grandchild, Sarah Olumayowa Mopelola who keeps me pretty busy, active, and healthy.

I am very grateful to Pastor Ghandi Olaoye, senior pastor of Redeemed Church, Jesus House DC, Silver Spring, Maryland, who, despite his busy schedule and missionary travels, found time to go through this book and write the "Foreward."

I acknowledge the efforts of Ms Darlene Demoss who typed the original script and also the efforts of Ms Ronke Shebanjo, my husband and my son who finally did the editing.

FOREWARD

This book presents to us, in a simplistic, Godly approach, matter-of-fact insight into the issue of why so many have left Africa, are leaving Africa, and desperately *wish* to leave Africa.

It renders a desperate, much needed awareness call to all direct and indirect descendants of Africa in all corners of the world to try to recover and replenish their fading heritage, tradition and culture by educating and re-educating themselves, and passing down these age-old values to the coming generations.

To thousands of second and third generation Africans, Africa is but a continent, a far- away land where nothing seems to go right and from whence thousands seem to flee. Their detachment to Africa stems far beyond an unwillingness to even contemplate living there. To them, not only is Africa problematic, impossible-to-rebound continent, but the values, cultures and traditions are also unfitting for the Western culture. For the sake of years to come, let every descendant of

Africa strive to pass down some values and customs of their fatherland, as agreeably, it is important to bind to, and have a link to our heritage. Remember, an acorn does not fall far from its tree.

This book will serve as an adventure into an African, and remind him/her the importance of making sure our offsprings understand the nature of being African.

Although the Western culture has introduced Africans to a more orderly, documented and increasingly technological approach to life and its conveniences, this culture has also been packaged with its more dangerous and highly devastating aspects. An essential purpose of this book is to reinforce the good values that stem from a heritage untapped by the modern issues of today's society, closely interlaced with Christian values: in an attempt to repress the ever-increasing doom that will eventually accompany the negative aspects of the Western culture.

Pastor Ghandi Olaoye

Contents

DEDICATION v

ABOUT THE AUTHOR vii

ACKNOWLEDGMENTS ix

FOREWARD xi

INTRODUCTION xv

1
LEAVING A HOMELAND 1
    EDUCATION 4
    JOB OPPORTUNITY 6
    ASYLUM SEEKERS 9
    MARRIAGE AND FAMILY 10
    GREED & FRAUD 11
    DIVERSITY IMMIGRANTS (LOTTERY) VISA 12
    SLAVERY 13
    PRAYER 17

2
LIFE IN HOMELAND 18
    FAMILY AND COMMUNITY 19
    TRADITION AND CUSTOM 22
    RELIGION AND CELEBRATION 24
    WORK AND LEISURE 28
    PRAYER 32

3
LIFE IN THE NEW LAND 33
    LAND OF FREEDOM AND OPPORTUNITY 37
    ADJUSTMENT AND ORIENTATION 41
    PRAYER 49

4
WHERE DOES HELP COME FROM: CREATOR 50
- STRAINS AND STRESSES 62
- PRAYER... 73
- UNANSWERED PRAYERS 76
- HOW TO PRAY 81
- HOW OFTEN TO PRAY 82
- ANSWERS TO PRAYERS 83
- PRACTICAL HELP TO PRAYER 86
- PRAYER... 90

5
CONFLICTING CULTURES 91
- PRAYER... 100

6
AFRICANS CAN INFLUENCE OTHERS IN GODLY VALUES 102
- LOVE OF FAMILY 103
- RESPECT OF ELDERS 109
- DRESSING 114
- FOOD 117
- TALENTS 120
- PRAYER 125

7
SAVED TO SERVE 126
- CONCLUDING PRAYER 138
- CONCLUSION 138

BIBLIOGRAPHY 141

INTRODUCTION

I felt compelled to write this book because the Holy Spirit inspired me that the publishing of this book could make a change for a better life for many immigrants. The book is specially written for African immigrants but immigrants of other races will also benefit from reading it.

Africa is a big continent and varied in cultures and religions. Africa consists of many nations and tribes; Africa is rich in history and myth, so many that it will take a whole library of books to write about her and her people. Since many people have done that already, I will only write about the common things that stand Africans up as unique creations of the God Almighty. It will be pointed out that the aspirations of every human being are basically the same; and that only the Creator can meet mankind at the point of need satisfactorily.

I was born, bred and cultured in Africa. Also, I was educated and skillfully trained in Africa. I went to England for further education and professional training, got married and worked there for some time. I came back to Africa to work, live and interact with my people. I raised children up in Africa. I have been to several countries in Africa, from Egypt to South Africa and from West to East Africa, interacting with the people and getting acquainted with some of their predicaments. I know why our people venture abroad. I have also traveled to many countries in Europe, some in the Middle East including the Holy Land. At present I live in the United States of America. I have seen and experienced many of the problems Africans have to face to fit into their new countries of abode. The adjustment may be easy for a few but for the majority it can be very challenging. The adjustment can be frustrating, at times depressing; but success is attainable. I mean success in the light of God, which is accompanied by peace and fulfillment.

    I believe that being out of Africa physically should endear our hearts to the homeland and also to our people. I believe that this endearment should propel us to seek for the spiritual and physical prosperity of our people in whatever way we can.

    God knows where we are at any given time and He wants us to function best there for His glory. 'Where there is no rule, there is no sin'. (Rom 3.20b) For freedom to be real, it must be governed by rules and regulations. In general, all laws of the Western culture are based on the Ten Commandments of God as revealed by the Holy Bible. World rulers are ordained by God in His omniscience appropriate to the times to fulfill His purpose. To live in peace and prosperity requires hard work, obedience to the laws of the land, studying the culture of the land, embodying that which is God-honoring, at the same time, drawing strength from your rich cultural heritage.

We are all on this planet to fulfill God's purpose. We need to inspect ourselves to see whether we are in His purpose and if we are not, then we need to find out His purpose for our lives. "Loving God and loving your neighbor", which is the basis of all God's laws, will be fulfilled by obeying His will for us and for the benefit of others. Irrespective of ones position or affluence one can always make a difference in the society. I pray that this book will be an eye opener to my readers, as well as a source of encouragement and empowerment for their future and that of others.

1

LEAVING A HOMELAND

The Bible says:
The earth is the Lord's and the fullness thereof, the world and they that dwell therein.
Psalm 24:1

Africa is a very large continent, a very substantial integral part of God's creation. When God created the earth, He said it was good. Like other creations of His, He loved Africa and all the fullness thereof, including the people. He endowed Africa with big rivers, luscious land with wonderful economics and edible plants and animals. There are myriads of minerals like gold, silver, diamonds, petroleum oil and gas, tin, copper, coal and much more, embedded in the soil of Africa. The weather in most of the area is nice and warm - suitable for the inhabitants. The people are strong, warm-hearted, family-oriented and fun loving. A curious reader may wonder why so many of the inhabitants choose to live outside Africa for the past few centuries.

God's purpose for mankind is perfect but in His omniscience, He gave mankind free will to make a choice between right and wrong, between love and hate, and between peace and war. He did not leave mankind in darkness, He gave them conscience and the knowledge of a Creator who demands accountability.

In the long history of civilizations and kingdoms and governments of Africa, several free choices made by leaders and rulers of African communities have had adverse effects on their people and their resources. External forces like colonialism; trade (particularly slave traders) missionaries (Christian and Muslims) have enforced their ideologies on the people of Africa. Greedy traders and merciless slave traders have taken the opportunity of prevailing circumstances to introduce strife and mistrust and tribal wars into the continent.

The introduction of Christian and Muslim education to the people has resulted in mixed blessings. The same boat that brought in the missionaries also brought alcohol, guns, gunpowder, and more destructive ammunition than the natives were accustomed to. By conquering the inhabitants, enforcing the foreign ways of ruling, suppression and feudalism, led to the differential spread of Islam and Christianity across the continent.

Africans who had experienced different stages of civilizations comparable with other races like the Asians,

Chinese and Europeans; became interrupted in their ways of life and drawn into compromising with stronger powers. Africa became partitioned by these foreign powers that became their colonial overlords. African rulers and kings were intimidated to give up their territories and kingdoms. The more vocal leaders were bribed and brainwashed to submission. Islamic and Christian education spread in different areas of the continent thus shaping the attitude, moral and culture of the people, depending on which religion was more dominant within the community.

All these influences of education, religion, trade, and colonization have taken their toll on the countries of Africa up to date, despite the political independence of these countries. Most of them remain financially dependent on their former colonial masters like England, France, Belgium, etc. Many ordinary Africans citizens became restless and subsequently ventured outside to meet their different needs and aspirations. There is no point of the globe where one will not find an African pursuing one career or the other. The world has become a global village.

The afore written piece is just to give a background history as to why Africans migrate to other places for peace of mind and to have a better life. This type of migration is not limited to Africans. Other races have had to migrate to other lands; hence, countries like Australia, New Zealand, Canada and the United States of America have become more diverse to accommodate new ethnic minorities from distant regions.

Felicia Oguntomilade

Many Africans migrate for different reasons that will be enumerated in this next segment of the book. The amazing thing about the Creator is that he knows where everybody is at any given time and can communicate with anyone willing to listen to Him for guidance. He has the whole world in His hand.

EDUCATION

Most Africans have discovered within the last century, the importance of education in their society. Those who were not opportuned to have an education moaned their situation and decided to give the best possible to their children. The educated ones like Nelson Mandela, Dr. Nnamdi Azikwe, Dr Nkrumah, Bishop Ajayi Crowder, Sekou Toure William Tubman, Wole Shoyinka, Chief Awolowo, Dr. Mbeki, and other renowned persons, made the difference in their societies. In order to have meaningful success in the present day generation, education is the most important qualification and ingredient. As a result of this hunger for better life and success, most families will go to any length to acquire a good education for themselves and theirs.

Most countries in Africa can give basic education to their citizens who can afford it. There are many universities and colleges of education in some African countries and not enough in others. Many universities in Africa, however, do not offer as many courses and disciplines to cover the goals of aspiring students especially in technical fields.

Economic and political instability in many African countries causes major interruptions in African universities, such that a normal three-year course could span up to six years or more. Those who can afford to go abroad will make that move in order to avoid the needless waste of years.

There are many aspiring students who need to work to fund their college education. Though they may be very willing, there is a shortage of job opportunities in these countries that record very high unemployment ratios. Where there *is* available work, there is another problem: the inflexibility of modern day academic programs in our countries means that an employed person might not even be able to attend school, because there is a shortage of evening and distance learning programs to suit this lifestyle. These types of students will struggle to pay for a ticket out of Africa in order to achieve their educational goals.

There are also some disciplines in which students need technologically advanced countries to obtain the necessary experience to qualify for graduation.

These are some of the attractions that make aspiring students venture abroad to accomplish their educational goal. Only the students who manage to cross over to their desired destination can tell of their experiences whether favorable or otherwise. There is no crown without a cross, but there is always a very present help if one has a relationship with the Helper, God.

Felicia Oguntomilade

JOB OPPORTUNITY

There has been a lot of instability in governments of African countries since former colonies of European countries obtained their political independence. Countries have been dependent on their former overlords; hence they are not economically independent. Many countries that had their economies based on agriculture during the colonial era were denied the transition into the more productive system of mechanized farming; they were also denied support to build factories to process farm produce. The farm products remained raw commodities for factories in the colonizer's home country.

Palm oil, Palm kernel, cocoa, cotton, coffee seed, tea, raw gold, copper, silver, manganese, leather, groundnut, timber, etc., were all shipped abroad by colonial masters for the economies of their own countries. Whatever was imported back as processed goods was sold exorbitantly to Africans who could afford them. The prices of raw materials were dictated and controlled by the colonial masters, thereby reducing the African producers to mere laborers for foreign economies. Africans did not benefit much for their labor.

Even today, most farms remain rural, mainly based on human labor and are very unappealing to young educated Africans who probably might have wanted to remain on the farms. The inability to improve these situations, because of lack of finances, propelled the majority of our educated hopefuls to the shores of more lucrative opportunities in other countries based in other continents. A few countries lucky enough to have discovered mineral oil rely on foreign firms for the development and management of these resources. The foreign firms determine the price of the oil, which is generally shipped back to their foreign countries, effectually doubling the benefits they receive from that which is found in African soil. Within the last fifty years, however, the Organization of Petroleum Exporting Countries (OPEC) has introduced some controlling measures in the pricing of the commodity.

Instabilities in political systems due to several coup-de-tats by the armies of numerous African countries have also served to ruin the already battered or slowly growing economies of the relevant countries. Corruption in governmental circles has sapped the economy and discouraged external trade and investment. Some Africans who were willing to make a change were not given the political muscle to achieve the change.

The result of all this evil is a stagnant economy, a lack of new jobs; and countless employed workers who were not regularly paid. Many more remained unemployed. Africans had to seek for their livelihood elsewhere.

The currencies in many African countries have been miserably devalued ("no thanks" to the International Monetary Fund, I.M.F). A college graduate can no more maintain a simple family; neither can he pay for the annual rent of an apartment comfortably. Basic infrastructures are not maintained and there is an excess insecurity for the safety of life and property owned in many cities. The outcome? Those people who have the will and the means to travel out venture to do so.

There are citizens of South Africa who had to go abroad to escape inhuman treatment and degrading labor by the apartheid white usurpers of the land and government. The white settlers thought they were superior beings, thus subjecting the natives to doldrums lives, forgetting that God created all humans equal.

The ethnic wars in Central Africa had ravaged the land and the people so much that there was no peace, no settlement and no plan for the future. It was such a hopeless situation for any economy, with the citizens having inadequate education and no security of tenure. Those who managed to escape from that country decided to remain abroad for their sanity and security.

Peace can only be found in the Prince of Peace. The warmongers and ethnic cleansers have no relationship with Christ, which in turn results in a lack of love for fellow Africans and no fear of God consequently resulting in the turmoil in that area of Africa.

In some relatively peaceful areas of West Africa like Nigeria, there are seasoned technocrats, teachers and various professional workers who by the age of sixty have to be retired according to the rule of government. Their pension fund cannot keep up with the rate of inflation and their normal standard of living. They are still very active mentally and physically and so many of them venture to work elsewhere abroad temporarily. This is a pitiable brain drain for Africa. Many Africans of this caliber end up working in the Middle East, Europe or America.

ASYLUM SEEKERS

Of recent in some African countries, tyrannical leaders who have become so dictatorial have emerged as head of governments or the armed forces. They cannot tolerate any opposition to their style of leadership. Prominent opposition members have been executed or incarcerated under one false accusation or the other. Their properties have been destroyed and their families live in fear. Some of them have to sneak abroad if they find a way of escape. They seek refuge in democratic countries where the government sympathizes with their plight and believes in the ideology of democracy.

Corruption has been enshrined in the running of some corporations, organizations, and institutions like the universities. There are some workers in these institutions who are not morally bankrupt and would not bend to lower their moral standards. They work according to their conscience. Such workers have been known to suffer persecution so seriously that they fear for their lives. Some flee to other countries, while the families they leave behind are haunted so vigorously that they too eventually seek refuge in other countries. The result is the breaking up of the complete family unit.

There are some of our people who have to flee because of persecution due to their faith. Some zealous intolerant Muslim leaders like Idi Amin of Uganda persecuted pastors and Christian families viciously. Some were executed, some incarcerated and dehumanized. Many who could escape to other countries did so instead of renouncing their faith. This example is not limited to Uganda alone, it happened in Sudan and subtly in other countries.

Thank God for the kind and democratic countries of the world that accommodate these creatures of God Almighty as asylum immigrants.

MARRIAGE AND FAMILY

Many immigrants from Africa desire to have spouses from their home country of origin for understandable reasons. For this purpose, desired spinsters migrate out to meet their spouses.

Some married couples separate, one spouse leaving the other at home to seek a better life temporarily for their families. After some time, the yearning for their family intensifies, and seeing that the situation at home has not changed economically, and security has not improved, they therefore decide to let their families join them.

There are parents of immigrants who need health care that is not available back home. Economic woe had impoverished the few hospitals. Doctors cannot work properly with outdated drugs and equipments. Hospital infrastructures have broken down. Unstable electricity and water supplies render making health practices unfeasible. Those who can afford it take their parents abroad for their health and maintenance.

Many children are born by immigrant Africans. These children become citizens of such countries. They remain there because they have better opportunities for life and development.

These are some of the reasons why families remain immigrants and settle in their new countries.

GREED & FRAUD

Africa is potentially very rich. It is proverbially a land that should be flowing with milk and honey. In one of the countries in West Africa, the head of the state was once quoted that his country had so much oil and money that he did not know what to do with it. Alas! Greed and fraud and mismanagement have devastated that country that many of her citizens can hardly afford three square meals a day, while a few are so rich that they store their loot in foreign banks. They live like kings and queens over and above hard working citizens. Some of these looters flee abroad to foreign land to enjoy their loot comfortably. Are they happy? Moral integrity is still valued in African basic culture. They cannot be really happy at home.

These "make believe" happy people encouraged some criminals to seek their own fortune illegally by trading in drugs, consequently a large percentage of these criminals make their homes in prisons abroad or die in the chase.

Proverbs 10:22 says:
The blessing of the Lord, it maketh rich,
and addeth no sorrow with it.

DIVERSITY IMMIGRANTS (LOTTERY) VISA

Hither to, traveling abroad has been limited to people who are in need of higher education, health care, family ties, jobs and the likes. In all these cases, people concerned have been further limited in their efforts by selective immigration rules of their desired country.

Of recent America has increased the number of immigrants from Africa through a wider umbrella of the Diversity Immigrants (lottery) visa for those who win the lottery and can afford the resultant cost of passage . This has encouraged people who would not have ventured to migrate to do so, because it is a chance for better prospects in life especially considering the poor financial and job situation within Africa . In this category of immigrants, there are doctors, pharmacists, nurses, accountants, teachers, lawyers, and technocrats, even people who have retired and still feel able to work. It is good for the individual but it is a big brain drain of highly qualified professionals from such African countries. This is one of the reasons why Africans should pray for the restoration of the land and for God-fearing leaders in each country so that people will be encouraged to stay at home and contribute their quota to the redevelopment of Africa.

SLAVERY

This unfortunate situation of the past cannot be ignored in this book because this historical horror had forced millions of Africans to leave their countries and become slaves. Their survivors have become citizens of various countries of the world by birth e.g. America, England, Caribbean countries, Canada, Brazil, etc. Most of these survivors of the forced immigrants have neither seen Africa nor lived there but they have African genes in them and African blood in their veins. Despite the survivors' inexperience of life in Africa, they still have a lot in common; therefore this book will be relevant to these survivors in many parts. These eminent sons and daughters of Africa passed through a lot of hardships, their cultures have been modified but they still maintain a distinct way of life different from other cultures around them. This cultural issue will be discussed in another chapter of this book. The fact that these groups of people are outside Africa is the relevance of this point.

Their forefathers and mothers have weathered horrible storms of labor and torture and degradation. They were transported inhumanely from Africa to whatever destination they were taken to for labor. They and their survivors have labored hard to maintain the economy of their forced masters. They almost had no right at all until God heard their cry and changed the heart of some head of government in Britain and America. They were convicted by the Holy Spirit to recognize their sinfulness and open their eyes to the light of truth and the slaves were freed. Gradually, by the anointing and endurance given by God to people like William Wilberforce, Abraham Lincoln and Rev. Martin Luther King and others, they overcame and became full citizens like other immigrants in these countries.

God remains faithful and listen to the cry of the oppressed like he heard the Israelites in Egypt and rescued them through Moses.

These immigrants have weathered the storms of leaving their homeland and the teething problem of adjusting to the "new land", but the cultural difference is still palpable in parts of the world like America, England, Canada, the Caribbean Islands and some in the Eastern world where traces of Africans have permanently resided.

God is a God of purpose and He has created man for a purpose in his life, no matter where one is in His created universe. For whatever purpose Africans leave their homeland, this purpose can only be achieved by knowing and acknowledging one's Creator, and having a relationship with Him on a personal basis. Whatever one has to go through, a believer will know that he is not alone and not desperate.

There is One greater than him that is with him and will see him through.

At this point readers, if you do not know your Creator and do not have a one-to-one relationship with His Son Jesus through whom you can reach Him, I invite you to His divine family by praying this prayer of acknowledging Him and surrendering to Him. You may think you do not need to, because you are smart and educated or that you are good enough to reach your human goal. What about your eternal goal? Nobody is good enough for that.

The period of one's sojourn in this life is a very short one compared to the time in eternity. What happens after death is as real as now. If you care for your life now, it is more expedient for you to care for your eternal life. Your "success" here, and how you attain it or how you do not attain it will dictate your destiny for eternity.

The Bible says in Heb. 9:27

> *And it is appointed unto men*
> *once to die,*
> *but after this the judgment.*

The Bible says in Rom. 3:20

> *For all have sinned, and come*
> *Short of the glory of God.*

Felicia Oguntomilade

In Romans 6:23

> *For the wages of sin is death;*
> *but the gift of God is eternal life*
> *through Jesus Christ our Lord.*

John 3:16 affirms

> *For God so loved the world*
> *he gave his only begotten*
> *Son, that whosoever believeth in him*
> *would not perish but have*
> *everlasting life.*

In the light of God's word and the realization of who you are, join in this prayer for your good.

O God, I realize I am a sinner. I am sorry for my sin. I am willing to turn from my sin and I am in need of a Savior. I receive Jesus Christ as my Savior. I confess you Jesus as Lord of my life. I want to follow you and let you lead me. I surrender my life to you now and forever. Amen.

If you heartily pray this prayer, it is a decision to surrender to the lord Jesus Christ and the beginning of a new life in Christ. You will grow gradually by communing with God daily and reading the word of God, which is the Bible.

African Immigrants

You cannot have a relationship if you are not on speaking terms with Him.

At the end of every chapter there will be a relevant prayer that I want every reader to participate in and adjust to his situation.

PRAYER

Dear Lord, I know I am here for a purpose. I know that you have a purpose for my life. I ask you Lord that you will direct my purpose to be in line with yours. Give me direction in all I think, speak or do. Let your grace accompany me in my life where I now reside. Lead me Lord, lead me in thy righteousness. Make thy way plain before my face: for it is thou Lord only, that can make me dwell in safety.

Thank you Lord for your love for me, and my kind in, Jesus name. Amen.

2

LIFE IN HOMELAND

Africa is a huge continent comprising of several nations. European colonial masters mostly created these nations; they partitioned the whole of Africa, turning it into a convenient division of their properties in order to claim their territory. This made administrative common sense to them but it divided some tribes, merging together incongruous ethnic groups, which has been a major source of conflict up to this day.

The people of Africa are so diverse in tribes, clan, religion and culture. These differences have so much impact on the social life of each individual group that it makes them distinct from one another. For the purpose of this book, I will not go into details of the individual groups; but in the diversity I intend to break down the general pattern of life in Africa. Africa is very rich in culture and religion, sensitive to moral standing and very community oriented.

Africans like other nations of the world have glorious past history of empire and dominions, kings and queens and dynasties that have been degraded or destroyed; but the spirit of the people cannot be killed. The people are conscious of who they are and proud of their heritage. This is being passed on progressively to their generations who are reviving what they can of their past. A lot have been written about the Zulu tribes and kingdom,the Pharaohs of Egypt, the Queen of Sheba and the Ethiopians, the Yoruba kingdom of great OBAS, the Benin and Edo Empire, the Fulani and Hausa empires ,and the Ashanti kingdom, just to name a few of the glorious past. Indeed Africa is rich in history.

FAMILY AND COMMUNITY

Most African families are patrilineal. A family consists of a head, which is usually a man, followed by a wife or wives, children, grandfathers and grandmothers, aunts, uncles and cousins. European culture and economic limitation have streamlined the usual big household into economically managed sizes. Religions like Christianity and Islam have also made some impact on the size of families. In general, children are produced and brought up under the influence of a father and mother joined together in marriage of some sort. It could be church marriage or marriage by Imam or pure native marriage according to custom. Children are greatly valued as a heritage from God and marriage is viewed to be more successful if blessed with children. Children are loved and nurtured by the whole family.

Discipline is an essential ingredient of upbringing because an ill-mannered or unruly child or grown up is a disgrace to the family. Male children are particularly welcomed as it is generally accepted that the male keeps up the family name and traditions to future generations. The female children are supposed to be married off and produce children for other families. This trend affected female education adversely before but this has changed for better. Male and female children that are educated can reach any high standard for which their parents can be proud of.

African families live in communities that are closely knitted together by land heritage, religious heritage, customs and social ties. Nobody is an island to himself - that is not Africa. People are usually committed to their kin and ethnic group; they try to stand by them through good times and bad times. This difference is felt as a social deficit when Africans are on their own outside Africa - it is like no man's land.

Age is well honored and respected in Africa. An elder woman or man is regarded as Papa or Mama if even they are not directly related. They are addressed with respect and never by first name. Children specially respect parents. In general these family principles are in conformity with the Bible doctrine.

1 Peter 5:6 says

> *Likewise ye younger, submit yourselves*
> *To the elder*
> i.e. respect the elders

Exodus 20:5 says

> *Honor thy father and thy mother;*
> *That thy days may be long upon*
> *The land which the Lord thy God giveth thee.*

Proverbs 19:18

> *Chasten (discipline) thy son while there is*
> *Hope, and let not thy soul spare*
> *For his crying.*

Most families attempt to give good education to their children so that their children may have good opportunities for progress in life. Family ambition ripples into community ambition as well because a successful son or daughter of the community is a pride of that community. Such successful children are supposed to attract good fortune to their fatherland.

Felicia Oguntomilade
TRADITION AND CUSTOM

Africans are very rich in tradition and custom. Every community has its own tradition linking them to their history, which may be written down or passed down orally through the elders from generation to generation. A country like Ghana, Nigeria, or Tanzania may each comprise of twenty or more tribes and each of these tribes can be broken down to several communities; one can only imagine the array of customs and traditions. These customs and traditions are very important to every individual as they shape their way of life and value.

This book is not meant to go into details of traditions and customs of Africa but to make the readers aware of why an African longs for home or what can make him happy or otherwise, or how he can relate with others to make for a fully abundant life away from home. This also relates to how he can feel fulfilled and be a blessing to others.

Everybody has a yearning and a hope to be successful and be fulfilled. It will be discovered as one matures that true success and fulfillment can only be achieved when one discovers one's purpose in life as designed by the Creator. This is enhanced by the fellowship and love we share with fellow human beings and the love we have for God. This is why Africans in their own ways are ardent worshipers and love fellowship with community members. Absence of this results in loneliness and feelings of not belonging when one is out of fellowship. It can also result in psychological ailment for immigrants who can be misunderstood and misdiagnosed.

It is part of African culture to be friendly and warm and sometimes loud in manifestation of the warmth. This can be communicated by different types of salutations, like handshakes, hugging and clear physical signs of reverence and respect.

There are different ways of addressing chiefs and elders, women and men, and also children. Every body is not greeted with "hello" or "hi."

Africans love titles, many expect to be addressed by their title which they work so hard to get. In some communities, it is a sign of respect for a younger person not to make eye contact with an older person while communicating with him or her. On the other hand, the Western culture may interpret that as dishonesty. Beware!

In Africa communication can be direct or indirect, it may be in parables and analogies, or in allegories depending on the wisdom and discretion of the communicator. Communication the 'African' way is implicitly accepted and response can be likewise.

There are also taboos in customs and languages:
- a younger person must know his limitation in the usage of proverbs when elders are present ;
- in order to maintain peace and mutual respect there is a limit to what one can say to in-laws or rival parties.

In rural areas, Africans are very welcoming. An appointment is not necessary to visit a friend or relative. Visitors are generally treated well.

There are myriads of African customs and traditions that can fill volumes of encyclopedias to list them; but suffice it to say that these customs and traditions shape the background of an individual African and reflects on his attitude to life in the land of immigration until changes gradually take effect, modifying a person's ways and lifestyles to suit new surroundings.

RELIGION AND CELEBRATION

From time eternal, man believes in the existence of a supreme being or beings to whom he is morally responsible and to whom propitiation need to be made.

This is very true of Africans. Africans are very moral in their thinking. They believe in "right" or "wrong" and they believe they can appease the gods by sacrificing one thing or the other for their wrongs.

There are so many gods, almost as many as there are tribal groupings. In addition to the god of their fathers, many Africans worship their departed or dead ones. Many look up to those spirits for guidance.

Egypt being an African country is a very good example as to various gods they worship as some were narrated in the Bible in the book of Exodus. Every plague that God inflicted upon the Egyptians when Pharaoh would not let the Israelites go to the Promised Land was directed against some prominent gods they worshiped. This is God manifesting to them that He alone is God and that no other god could stand his wrath.

Below are some gods of the polytheistic Egypt and the repercussions to the Egyptians worshipping them in share disregard to the true God, Jehovah Elohim for in Ex.12:12(b) the Jehovah God had promised:

And against all the gods of Egypt I will

execute judgements: I am the Lord

- He beshamed **Knam and Osiris** the gods of the Nile by turning the water of the Nile into blood;
- He rendered **Heqt,** the frog god, powerless, by turning on the plague of frogs to torment the Egypians through out all the land;
- He made ineffective the god of **mosquitoes and lice** by infecting all Egypt with the plague of mosquitoes and gnats and lice;
- He rendered inefficient the **god of flies** by causing the plague of flies all over Egypt;
- He belittled and beshamed **Hather** the goddess of cows and cattle by causing the diseases of boils and hail upon all the animals of Egypt; .
- He similarly rendered useless **Imhotep**, the god of medicine, by making sure that the medicine did not perform any healing to the cattle and beasts;and could not stop the plague of boils;

- Similarly **Isis,** the god of life did not perform nor restore life to the "dead" because Jehovah God had made **Isis** ineffective;
- In exactly the same way, Jehovah had beshamed and belittled **Isis the god of life, Nut, the sky goddess, Seth, the protector of crops, for He had used Locust to destroy crops** all over Egypt
- He Jehovah God had beshamed and rendered useless both Atem and Honus, the gods of light and darkness for Jehovah caused all darkness all over Egypt;
- He had beshamed **Osiris, the god of life** in that, in the meantime, Jehovah had instructed an angel of destruction to go into the houses of the Egyptians to kill their first borns, for it is these first borns that would become the priests respectively of the family's gods.

Thus the eternal God of gods executed judgement over the feable and powerless gods of Egypt..

There were many other gods in Egypt but not as important as those mentioned in the Bible. Like the Athenians of old, Africans have gods for every season, for drought, for rain, for mountains, for rivers, for sun, for thunder, for productivity, for iron and even for devil or Satan whom some worship and appease.

Today most Africans are either Christians or Muslims by faith whilst some others still hold on to the faith of their ancestors. You can hardly find an atheist in Africa. The fear of God or gods is apparent in their culture. Africans worship with songs and dances. Ceremony is attached to the worship with drums, musical instruments, clapping and merriment.

Ceremony is not limited to worship alone. Africans enjoy ceremonies. Africans celebrate childbirth, naming, marriage, engagement, chieftaincy, graduation, birthdays, housewarming, death and burial, memorials, etc. This mode of ceremonies has rippled into the spiritual life of Christians and Muslims, hence there is a lot of singing and dancing and clapping in African churches and in some mosques. It is part of life in Africa and it is scriptural to worship in this manner as advocated by David, who was an ardent praiser-and-worshiper of the God Almighty. The difference that each worshiper must identify is 'Who' is being worshiped? Is it the God Almighty or is it some pseudo-gods or some pagan gods ?

Psalm 150 reads:

> *Praise ye the Lord, Praise God in his*
> *sanctuary; praise him in the firmament of his power*
> *Praise him for his mighty acts;*
> *Praise him according to his excellent greatness;*
> *Praise him with the sound of the trumpet;*
> *Praise him with the psaltery and harp*
> *Praise him with the timbrel and dance;*

Praise him with the stringed instrument and organs
Praise him upon the loud cymbals;
Praise him upon the high sounding cymbals;
Let everything that hath breath
Praise the Lord.

Prayer, adoration and praise are elements of worship in Africa. Fear of the gods call for sacrifice, incantation and adoration to appease them. Some of these are manifested in African churches where prayer, praising, and physical show of dancing, drumming, clapping, singing and sometimes feasting are exhibited.

Initiation ceremonies are rampart in African tradition. It marks transition to adulthood, transition to cult membership, transition to chieftaincy or head of clan, transition to certain positions of power. Some initiation ceremonies are done in secrecy like in cult, some openly like in adulthood. Africans like to be recognized hence many work hard to attain and sustain recognition in society and pass same down to their descendants.

WORK AND LEISURE

Africans are traditionally hard working people. They despise laziness. They believe in sowing and reaping. They believe in achievement through hard work.

Farming and hunting are the earliest known occupations to man and most especially in Africa. Farming is treated both as a family joint activity as well as individual activity. Some communities help each other in tilling the ground and harvesting the crops according to farming seasons. Strength of the family used to be assessed by the size of their farms and the richness of their harvest.

Animal husbandry is another common profession in many parts of Africa especially in the savannah region. On a small scale, every family participates in animal husbandry - from rearing few goats and sheep to chicken and duckling around the homestead.

There are hunters who were the original butchermen. This profession remains in families and is revered. Many traditional family names and worship are associated with this calling. Many in this profession are heads of communities and local armies. They lead in the worship of the god of iron, which is associated with weapons of war, such as swords, cutlasses, sickles, knives, bows and arrows etc.

There are craftsmen and women according to the needs of communities e.g., goldsmith, carvers, blacksmith, weavers, tailors, barbers, hairdressers, caterers, dyers etc.

In areas near the rivers or seas, there are fishermen, net makers, boat builders, fish dryers, medicine makers etc.

In this modern era, these various professions have evolved with technology and the people are proactive with time and still very hard working. They have been replaced with engineers, doctors, architects, lawyers, nurses, teachers and technocrats in all spheres of enterprise. There are some factories, oilrigs, mechanized large farms and big time traders as well as petty traders. In some countries like Nigeria, there are more professionals than needed. Countries like South Africa who need to replace departing Europeans who cannot fathom equality with indigenous Africans are now benefiting from these professionals.

Africans have long been wonderful administrators as can be divulged from their history books; how they ruled kingdoms and empires until foreign interference destabilized the formal culture and politics of the native people. Today those instincts coupled with formal training do produce some very fine administrators; whereas some instincts plus greed and seared conscience have produced dictators and fraudulent politicians of diverse shades and exploitive capabilities.

Africans have produced warriors through out the ages - proud and fearless fighters who would fight any course to preserve their family and communities.

Africans work hard but at the same time, being very social people, they always find time for leisure. The elderly ones like to tell stories and narrate history in the evening over local wine and cola nuts. All work and no leisure make life dull and uninteresting. The end of a harvest season is a time for merriment and show-off. It is time for building and for prestige purchasing; time for weddings and for thanksgiving;it is time for giving praises for various blessings enjoyed in the past season. It is time for remembering the dead ones and to celebrate clan festivals; age group festivals and other similar festivities.

Introduction (engagement) and marriage ceremonies are elaborate especially in rich families. Some communities have a common festival when all the young men take their bride with pomp and merriment for all.

Modernity has brought more ideas to cultural leisure of Africans. There are more social, sports, and trade clubs which are also avenues for leisure.

Life in the homeland can be very full, warm and buoyant in time of peace. The type of community and the individuals or prevailing faith of the people can be a strong influence on the buoyancy. The social aspect of home life can be very attractive and can create a lot of nostalgia for Africans living abroad. This nostalgia can be balanced up by reflecting back on why such Africans left home in the first place; thereby creating a desire for an emigrant African to be grateful to God and to make a fresh determination to pursue those goals that will enable him or her to make a difference in the community at home and wherever he or she resides.

Phillipians 4:13 says:

> *I can do all things through*
> *Christ which strengthens me.*

Felicia Oguntomilade
PRAYER

Lord, I thank you for my homeland. I thank you for the opportunity you have given me to be where I am.

I know that you are sovereign over all the nations and you are present everywhere.

I know you are aware of my situation and I appreciate your love for me.

I ask you Lord to be a light to my path and direction to my life.

I need your grace all the time to perfect all that concerns me.

Mold me for your purpose and make me a blessing to others in Jesus name I pray. Amen.

3

LIFE IN THE NEW LAND

It takes a lot of courage, determination and sentiment to make a decision to leave the homeland for whatever reason. Many people evaluated the pros and the cons before making that decision and therefore prepare for whatever it takes to make it in the new land. Many endeavor to escape from situations in the homeland and therefore prepare to endure whatever they need to confront in the land of refuge or the new land of opportunities. Many desperate job seekers left, seeking for an opportunity to make a living - no matter what the type of job, but alas, after the first few months, they realize that the opportunities available are not the best.

Many have heard of people or seen people who have successfully lived satisfactory lives abroad and have therefore longed for such opportunities; not knowing what it takes for such people to accomplish their seemingly desired goal.

Many reached their newfound land before they realize how different people can be from their own people back home. The difference is not only in color but also in attitude, in culture, in language, in education and in values. There are countries with mixed values and mixed cultures and mixed religions and sometimes it can be very confusing. America (U.S.A.), which had been a country of immigrants and therefore is peopled from all corners of the globe, is typical; a newcomer will find these mixed cultures depending on where he works, or who he works for, and depending on where he resides.

Some countries are more welcoming than others depending on the policy of the government towards immigrants or visitors.

This situation is not unique to Africans alone. The whole created earth; the entire globe is filled with human race by migration or by immigration since that time of dispersion at Babel in the account written in the Bible in Genesis chapter 11, verses 1 to 10.

Quote from Verses 8 and 9:
So the Lord scattered them abroad
from thence upon the face of all the
earth; and they left off to build
the city.

Therefore is the name of it called
Babel; because the Lord did there
confound the language of all the earth

and from hence did the Lord scatter them abroad upon the face of all the earth.

Other countries outside the continent of Africa have had similar situations in their history; whereby their people have had causes to migrate to other countries. The Jews at the time of captivity by Nebuchadnezar (586BC) or at the time of the Holocaust in Germany, have had to flee to other lands. The Irish people had to migrate at times of the potato famine, religious oppression and political unrest. The English under similar oppressive situations had to flee from their nation for religious freedom; and they formed the initial immigrants in New England in what is now known as the United States of America displacing some Native Americans in the 16th century. Other nationalities all over Europe subsequently migrated to the U.S.A. for various other reasons. World history is full of adventurers, fortune seekers, empire builders and missionaries who have shaped history and geography and some have reaped souls for Christ while others have spread terror and hatred in the name of some other religion. .

Over the years, the adventure became a disaster to some and for so many others it was a success story but only with hard work and faith in a trustworthy God. Others followed to build on, or to reap, the success of the hard working pioneers.

Felicia Oguntomilade

Over viewing the history of immigration in America, Roger Daniels wrote:[1]

> Coming to America whether as a sojourner or as a settler, was in many cases to partake in an adventure, a drama, even a dream. For many the adventure became a disaster, the drama a tragedy, the dream a nightmare. Not all the individual stories have a happy ending...............
>
> Too often in writing about immigrants, we forget that there were immigrant losers as well as winners, and that sometimes "winning" took generations to achieve. Despite these and other negatives, American immigration was and is overall a success.

The above quoted passage referred to initial pioneers of America but the truth remains the same virtually today for any immigrant to any country. The differences in the outcome of the adventure, I believe, depends on the adventurer's purpose, his level of faith in a trustworthy and covenant God who can make His grace abound for those who trust in Him.

---

[1] Coming to America by Roger Daniels, Page 28, copyright 1990 by Visual Education Corporation.

LAND OF FREEDOM AND OPPORTUNITY

In the past forty years i.e. from the 1960s, many Africans have seen America, England, Canada and other parts of Europe as lands of freedom and opportunity. This is more so because of the prevailing conditions building up in some African countries; the political witch hunting by tyrants like Idi Amin of Uganda, Abacha of Nigeria, Vervowed in South Africa. The instability of coups and counter coups in some countries in West Africa, the ethnic cleansing in Central Africa and the effect of I.M.F. on the economy of third world countries are other reasons why Africans view other lands as lands of freedom.

These lands of "freedom and opportunity' are what they are today from years of hard work, slavery, wars, trial and error, and pages of legislation drawn to protect what has seemingly been achieved. The rules and regulations of such countries were enforced to prevent anarchy, to maintain their economic standard, to protect their freedom and the health of their citizens.

Human prejudice on one hand plus a country's determination to maintain set standards on the other hand, could cause immigrants to face series of problems and antagonism sometimes difficult for them to comprehend. This is again not limited to African immigrants but it is sometimes more greatly enforced on Africans because of racial prejudice. Racial prejudice is not written anywhere but it is often implicitly noticed in housing, job searching and job evaluation: situations where Africans are the needy party.

Asian Americans faced similar problems of integration for many years before they began to be recognized. The Asian persevered; worked at these problems and eventually resorted to self-support their race, thereby growing into communities of their own within the big cities of the world. They established businesses of their own, creating employment for their own immigrant people. They took advantage of Americans' greatest civic resources, its schools and universities to improve themselves and to get accustomed to American ways before they could integrate gradually into the society. Many of them were well qualified before they migrated but that did not qualify them for America or for England or any other European country. Currently in many major cities in the Western world, there exist 'China Towns' or Eastern communities.

The Jews have experienced persecution, immigration problems, and prejudice more than any other race in the whole world. Most of them are highly cultured and well educated. Their laws and education have been the bedrock of civilization, as we know it today; yet their difficult experience of getting accepted and integrated into every society outside their own is a wealth of knowledge for immigrants from Africa. They still maintain their culture and adjust or complement their education with whichever society they come into. Jews in America for example had a long history before they became who they are today. When they fled from countries where they were horribly persecuted, they left their riches behind to save their lives. Many had small beginnings: itinerant traders on horses and carts with their wares to meet the needs of the community they lived in. The generation of such itinerant traders now owns some of the largest department stores and corporations known today in America. They made wonderful use of their freedom and opportunity to reach where they are today in countries such as America, England and Canada. The Jews worked hard, did not mind how low they began but sure persevered. In addition, they have a covenant with God who never goes back on his promise for them.

The Irish too had their difficult past in settling down and being accepted in America,. the fact that they were white and that they were Europeans not withstanding. The old prejudice of the Irish by the English still haunted them. The harsh immigration control was fully applied to them. Many of the Irish people left their country because of scarcity of food and provision at a point in time, others because of religious persecution, others were exiled, and many more wanted freedom from their lords and masters in their own country. America then was advertised as land without landlords. Land was available for those who wanted ownership. The Irish came to America in millions, they had their teething period. Many did menial jobs and were not fully integrated into elite society. They learnt various types of tactics in order to survive.

The German immigrants also had the experience in learning the American culture and language and also "stooping to conquer" their initial difficulties by yielding quietly to the ways of earlier immigrants that were mainly English. Many of the early immigrants from Europe did not come voluntarily; their immigration was almost like those of the slaves from Africa, though they were not called slaves. They were indentured servants who became free after serving some years of agreement. Some Germans were forced to migrate as a replacement for punishment for their crimes in their home country.

From some of these narrations, one can see a general picture of immigrants to America from various countries at different times. This classifies America as a country of various immigrants, except for the few American Native Indians surviving their destabilization.

America is a very large multi-ethnic, multicultural, multi- linguistic country that has worked hard and had fought relentlessly for freedom for its citizens. (English is the official language) It is a very rich ,advanced ,democratic country , Because of her history, it has become sympathetic towards the oppressed and persecuted people of the third world countries. It is a country with diverse cultures - as diverse as the people now inhabiting the country. The Constitution grants equality to all its citizens.

Every immigrant of whatever race or culture has a unique tale to tell about his or her experience in the process of integrating into the society of residence. Here is one told by a Mexican immigrant:[2]

> America is a very interesting place.
> Mixed in contradiction, it is as beautiful as
> it is ugly, as objective as it is closed.
> Many adjectives describe the America
> I know. America greets its Immigrant in different
>> ways; Some are received with open arms,
>> jobs and appreciation; others are not. America
>> does not blatantly display the type of
>> policy that requires newcomers to walk
>> through filth to get to their goal, but it happens.

This impression is very true in many circumstances depending on the goal of the individual. Having passed through some harrowing tests and demeaning jobs, and obtaining the cultural literacy experience; the sky is the limit of any immigrant's rise depending on his individual zeal and hard work. The answer is "Adjustment and Orientation".

ADJUSTMENT AND ORIENTATION

Most Africans who have ventured to settle in America temporarily or permanently are educated to a minimum qualification for employment to say the least. Many of them are highly educated with two or three degrees, some having

---

[2] Fifty years in America through the Back Door, Elena Caceres

been professionals in their countries of origin. When these Africans arrive at their chosen destination, be it America, Canada, England or any other first world country, they realize that they are not automatically qualified to enter into the same status of jobs they were educated for back home in Africa. Degrees from third world countries have to be assessed by delegated authorities of first world countries. Even when it is accepted to be fair degree, most times, it does not qualify the owner for job automatically.

It is necessary for any newcomer to check on employment requirements in the range of his or her qualifications; if the applicant is lucky enough he or she should take what immediate employment opportunity that can be grabbed; if not some alternative employment in the same range in another realm should be pursued; in the meantime the applicant can make efforts to upgrade his or her qualification for his preferred choice of carrer

Professionals from other countries will have to take professional examinations of the new country of abode before they are allowed to practice. To successfully pass these examinations, it is necessary to attend accredited schools whose fees are usually exorbitant. Consequently a professional new comer may need to take up some form of temporary employment in order to save up for the professinal examination fees and additionally maintain body and soul and also keep the family happy .. It is generally believed that the purpose of this examination is not only to bring the newcomer up to professional standard but also to limit competition with home professionals; this gimik is part of the price to be paid for daring to come and live and work in another man's country.

In some instances a new immigrant may need to start afresh and undertake training and academic education for his trade or profession, an idea that is well taken only if the cost is affordable perhaps through sponsorship by some kind organisation, otherwise, the immigrant has to study part- time and work full time to pay the fees. Sponsorship and loans are not easily available to new immigrants..

Education in many African countries is basically book knowledge because of the technical limitations of the society. In America for instance, part of the education is cultural, technical, societal and experiential. A person with African orientation may need a period of re-orientation into a new land before he can understand the new societal mode of thinking, values, economy and work ethics, and even relaxation patterns. Jobs and economy float around these silent essential orientations.

A fresh immigrant must be aware of the type of job opportunities around the part of the country where he wants to settle before embarking on a line of training to be acquired in order to avoid early destabilization and fraustration. This knowledge of such needed job opportunities can be researched by checking the Internet, asking relevant questions, checking the job market, etc. The new immigrant does not isolate himself or herself; applicants must learn to look, listen and be proactive for necessary awareness of job opportunities

There are many immigrants who were good artisans, caterers, tailors and traders in their home country. These endeavors can still be a good source of income to them in a new country of abode if they reside in a location where their trade can be easily marketed. A good tailor can earn a reasonable living if he stays where there are many of his countrymen and women, like the Chinese and Koreans do. There are many African Americans who just love African attire for occasions like wedding and house-warming, etc.. African tailors can establish tailoring businesses in strategic locations where aspiring African American residents can reach out for their fancies;

Similarly a good cook can do the same if she advertises her trade locally. Every body likes good food. The Indians and the Chinese, the French and the Italians are very much in that business..

Since it is a world of human beings, most trades, arts and other occupations can be modified and improved upon to fit the community one resides in.

Adjustment is not limited to jobs, trade and occupations alone. Many people arrive in a new country as visitors and then later make up their minds to stay either temporarily or permanently. A very important adjustment that has to be made: is the visa status. This is of absolute necessity for peace of mind.. New immigrants should immediately find out and check with friends how to go about effecting the correct status of their visas. Immigration lawyers specialize in working on options that can help with visa adjustments of various classes. Immigrants should not wait until the expiration date on the visa before making necessary adjustments or else it will be a cat- and -mouse issue with the authorities. It may be pertinent to mention here that a student visa does not automatically adjust to work visa; a work permit is required. Initially a temporary work permit can progress to other desirable status if necessary guidelines are followed.

Recently the Diversity immigrants (lottery) visa that leads to permanent resident visa has been another channel of entry for many immigrants. After five years of maintaining good residential status, a permanent resident can gain the coveted citizenship status after going through the necessary procedures. Whatever regulation applies to one's visa must be noted and abided by, otherwise the residency can be jeopardized and deportation will imminently follow. Immigrants are advised not to overstay their welcome.

An aspect of adjustment is the responsibility of bringing up children to fit into the new society; and yet it is essential to instill the right values and the fear of the Lord into them. Back home it is the duty of everybody around the child to see that a child is properly brought up. In the new land both parents may be so involved in working and making some reasonable living that they inadvertently neglect their children who more than ever need parental guidance and support to maintain the children's confidence. Schools or daycares are not equipped to do much nor to discipline foreign children; as parental values fall very low on their list of services. Children tend to imbibe just what they see others do, good or not-so-good..

There is a vital cultural adjustment that is essential for Africans to make in their countries of immigration :It is an accepted cultural and Biblical fact that the man is the head of the family. He should be expected to provide for the family. The leadership of the family does not depend on whether the wife or the husband makes more money. The headship is unchangeable by any circumstances. The headship is spiritual in nature and it is only common sense, since only one master can lead without confusion. The children must be brought up under this leadership. It is also reasonable pride for the man to provide for the family, BUT if by any circumstance, the woman is blessed to bring in more money to the home, that does not change her role of acknowledging the headship of her husband within the family. The headship role is not a master –to- servant role; it is a mutual loving administrative role for smooth relationship in the family. By wisdom the woman builds her home.
Proverb 14:1 says,

> *Every wise woman buildeth her house;*
> *but the foolish plucketh it down*
> *with her hands.*

The husband's role is not limited to the weight of the pay packet. He should not be resentful, nor should he be lazy. He should endeavor to improve himself if necessary and be proactive at home. He should not allow cultural pride to overrule his sensibility. He should appreciate and love the wife and accept who she is; a helpmeet, and be grateful to God for the provision of such a helpmeet. He must recognize his God-given leadership under Christ in the family. Role is not reversed. He as a loving husband will need to accomplish the smooth running of the family by taking children to school, helping with homework and doing whatever needs to be done when his wife is away at work. Chores can be shared. Some men are even better cooks while some women, when they are available, will take pride in cooking No chore is out of bound for any couple in love. Children must be brought up to do chores appropriate for their age.

If the husbands love their wives as Christ loves the church, husbands will do anything, with love., for their wives Hardly can one find a woman who will not respond to love.

Circumstances differ from family to family; there is no reason for comparison or to allow interference of relatives or friends in to this "mystery" of marriage. It is between husband and wife as ordained by God. If both are believers, any problem in the union should be taken to the Originator who is Christ. He will see the couple through.

In adjusting to a new land, the reader should reflect on Psalm 37:3-5

Trust in the Lord and do good;
so shalt thou dwell in the land,
and verily thou shall be fed.
Delight thyself also in the Lord;
and he shall give thee the desire
of thine heart.
Commit thy way unto the Lord;
trust also in Him; and he shall
bring it to pass.

Also the reader should think on Psalm 24:1

The earth is the Lord's and the
fullness thereof; the world, and they
that dwell therein.

The Lord knows the strains and stresses that strangers to new lands have to go through. He will be with his people and uphold them and give the comfort they need especially if they ask Him.

PRAYER

Dear Lord and Father, I thank you for who you are.

I thank you for you are able to do all things because you are almighty.

There is nothing hidden from you and there is no impossibility with you.

I surrender every aspect of my life to you for your guidance and direction.

Show me your way to lead my life.

Give me uncommon favor so that I shall flow into your grace in whatever circumstance I am in. (You can mention your own special circumstances.)

Direct my path and lead me to the type of success that comes from you.

Open your way for me in circumstances that seemed blocked to man.

The glory shall be yours only as I pray this in Jesus Name. Amen.

4

WHERE DOES HELP COME FROM: CREATOR

Life is a pilgrimage. It is a pilgrimage with a purpose, a divine purpose. It is therefore necessary to know the diviner in order to be acquainted with his ways, his character, and his power. A relationship with this diviner, who is the creator of all that exist, will enlighten a believer as to the purpose of his existence and how to achieve it.

Someone like Charles Darwin will like us to believe that we evolved from apes; it is a lie from the devil. It is as humanistic as those who think that they can clone themselves and live forever, of course that will be eternal life in hell fire. Man is not here by accident or chance. God creates man for his glory. He knew us before we were born.

David wrote psalm 139 as inspired by God.

Verses 13-16:
For thou has possessed my reins;
thou hast covered me in my mother's womb.
I will praise thee, for I am fearfully
and wonderfully made
marvelous are thy works
and that my soul knoweth right well.

My substance was not hid from thee, when I
was made in secret, and curiously wrought
in the lowest part of the earth.
Thine eyes did see my substance, yet
being imperfect: and in thy book all
my members were written,
which in continuance were fashioned,
when as yet there was none of them.

When God called Jeremiah to be the prophet as divinely ordained, he was told by God in Jeremiah 1:4;
Before I formed thee in the belly, I
knew thee; and before thou comest out
of the womb, I sanctified thee, and
I ordained thee a prophet unto the nations.

The word of God confirms that He created us, and that He has a purpose for every creature of His. If a life is lived according to God's purpose in whatever profession or calling in life, that life will glorify God.

Who is this God? Remember Pharaoh of Egypt asked that same question from Moses when Moses asked for the release of the Israelites from Egypt to worship the Lord:

> Ex 5:2
>
> *And Pharaoh said, Who is the Lord that I should obey his voice to let Israel go? I know not the Lord, neither will I let Israel go.*

Pharaoh trusted in the gods of Egypt so much that he became insolent to the God of gods therefore; the ten plagues that the Lord inflicted on the Egyptians were aimed at the gods of Egypt (Ex 12:12(b)) in order to shame the gods and let Pharaoh know who is the only Lord God

Nebuchadnezar was smitten with a mental disease in which the Bible recorded that he became like a beast for seven seasons before he eventually acknowledged who God is, and the limitless extent of God's power .

Daniel 4: 34-35 says it all:

> *And at the end of the days I,*
> *Nebuchadnezar lifted up mine eyes unto heaven,*
> *And my understanding returned unto me;*
> *And I blessed the Lord Most*
> *High, and I praised and honored Him*

That liveth forever, whose dominion
Is everlasting dominion and his
Kingdom is from generation to generation.
And all inhabitants of the earth are
Reputed as nothing; and he doeth
According to his will in the Army of heaven
And among the inhabitants of the earth;
And none can stay his hand,
Or say unto him, "What doest thou?"

An earthly king had to bow to the will of his Creator and also realize that all power, honor, riches and glory belong only to God alone..

The simple fact is that there is no atheist in the foxhole. People cry out to God automatically when in danger or point of calamity ; they cry out to God for deliverance without any prompting from anyone.

Many Christians have had several experiences with fellow travelers in the airplane. Some have tried to explain the term "being born again", to fellow passengers,, people who were apparently not interested in such scriptural topics ; but as soon as the plane showed some sign of turbulence that got passengers perplexed, a lot of the passengers suddenly got interested in the topic. Many who were not in the habit of praying started praying seriously for safety of the plane and passengers. The terrible incident of September 11th -2001 in America turned many hearts towards God and many did appreciate how short and fragile this human life could be.

People may flunctuate in their soul and spirit, depending on circumstances of their lives; but God, Father of the Lord Jesus Christ, His Son Jesus, the Holy Spirit i.e., the Trinity God, never change. He is the Almighty God who has revealed himself to humans in Romans 1:19-25:

> *Because that which may be known of God is manifest*
> *In them: for God hath shewn it unto them.*
> *For the invisible things of him from the*
> *Creation of the world are clearly seen, being understood*
> *By the things that are made, even his eternal power*
> *And Godhead: so that they are without excuse:*
> *Because that, when they knew God, they glorified*
> *Him not as God, neither were thankful; but*
> *Became vain in their imagination, and their foolish*
> *Heart remain darkened.*

(Remember Charles Darwin)

> *Professing themselves to be wise, they became fools,*
> *And changed the glory of the incorruptible God*
> *Into an image made like to corruptible man, and*
> *To birds and four footed beasts and creeping*
> *Things.* (Remember the golden calf etc.)
> *Wherefore God also gave them up to uncleanliness*
> *Through the lust of their own heart to dishonor*

Their own bodies between themselves;
Who changed the truth of God into a lie, and
Worshiped and serve the creature more than the
Creator, who is blessed forever. Amen.

This God of the Bible, the Creator of Man has wonderful attributes. The knowledge of the truth of God leads to godliness. Highlighting these attributes will encourage the reader to decide whom he can trust or whom to have faith in, and who to absolutely rely upon for help.

The Bible reveals that:

God is Love:

St John 3:16:specifically specifies:

For God so loved the world that he
Gave his only begotten Son, that whosoever
Believeth in him should not perish but have
Everlasting life.

2 John 4:7-10 also tells the world of the love of God and that His very nature is Love.

There was a period in my life that I felt low and unloved. God manifested love to me personally in a small still voice saying **'God is Love.'** This spiritual manifestation changed my feeling and attitude dramatically and I felt whole and healed

Another attribute of God is **Righteousness**

God is always right and fair in whatever He does. Psalm 147:5 declares this:

The Lord is righteous in all his ways
and holy in all his works

Deuteronomy 32:4 also reads:

He is the rock, his work is perfect: for
all his ways are judgement: a God of truth
and without iniquity, just and right is he.

In contrast to God's perfect righteousness, Isaiah 64:6 states that man's righteousness is as filthy rags, nevertheless, man need not get despondent because God is love, and for that course, he sent his Son Jesus Christ to the cross to deliver believers from their imperfection. This is why every man must accept and appreciate the Salvific works done by Jesus blood..

Another attribute of God is his **Holiness**. God is absolutely holy, spotlessly clean and undefiled. Moses was confronted with God's holiness in Exodus 3: 2-6. Isaiah had an awesome experience of God's holiness as recorded in Isaiah 6: 1-3. God cannot tolerate sin and yet he loves the sinner. Sin results in death, which is eternal death in hell, for the wages of sin is death.! He made a way of escape for believers in making his holy son pay for human sin; it is amazing as only God can sacrifice His only begotten son to appease (propitiate.) Himself to be able to forgive Man's sins What a grace! What a love!

Revelation 4: 8-11 reveals how the hosts of heaven acclaimed God's holiness and worship him. The same passage reveals what purpose man was created to fulfill.

A further attribute of God is His **Mercy**
Psalm 89:14 declares:
Justice and judgement are the habitation
of thy throne, mercy and truth shall
go before thy face.

Romans 3:26 reads:
To declare I say at this time his righteousness;
that he might be just and the justifier of him
which believeth in Jesus.

Christians are therefore justified by faith in Jesus who by love and mercy paid the penalty of sin.

Another Attribute of God is His **Truth**
His truth is revealed throughout the scripture and His son which reveals the Father as is declared in John 14:6:
I am the Way the Truth and the Life.

He told his disciples that if they had seen Him they have seen the Father.
Deuteronomy 32: 3-4 shows how Moses declares:
Because I will publish the name of the Lord;
ascribe ye greatness to our God

> *He is the Rock, his work is perfect;*
> *for all his ways are judgement, a God*
> *of* **Truth and without iniquity;** *just*
> *and right is he.*

GOD is **immutable**

He is constant and unchanging as declared by James 1:17:

> *Every good gift and every perfect*
> *gift cometh down from the*
> *Father of lights with whom is no*
> *variableness.*

Hebrew 13:5 declares:

> *Jesus Christ the same yesterday and today and forever.*

God does not need to change any plan of his because he knows the end from **before** the beginning. His purpose never changes. We can rely on his love and care at all times if even we cannot fathom it because of our limitations and our circumstances.

GOD is **Sovereign**

He reigns over all, irrespective of place and time or season . We might think that if He is sovereign, why is evil so rampant? Evil is subject to God's limitation. He is not to blame for the evil in the world for Satan has usurped the kingdom of the world for a time. God has permitted him,as an agent of God, to operate within certain boundaries; and this is to provide opportunity for man to freely use his freewill, and decide whether or not to yield to satan . This persecution is temporary until the final judgement when God will fix him and his cohorts in their final destination the lake of fire burning with brimstone . The Devil knows this and he is desperate hence his attack on man. No evil can overcome a child of God if he constantly dwell in that secret place of God's most High (Psalm 91).

GOD is **ominiscient**

He knows all; nothing comes to Him by surprise. This is a fallout of His eternal decree, for nothing happens unless he ordains it. Before it happens He knows it and may reveal it if He wants. If one can discern the scripture rightly, all that is happening in the world today has been long foretold.

Romans 11:33,36

O the depth of the riches both of the
wisdom and knowledge of God! How
unsearchable are his judgments,
and his ways past finding out.
For of him, and through him, and
to him are all things; to whom
be glory forever.

GOD is **ominipresent**

He is present everywhere at the same time   He was with Daniel in the lion's den. He saw Jonah in the belly of the fish. He was with the three Hebrew men in Nebuchadnazzer's furnace to ensure they were not burned. The presence of God in David's life led him to acknowledge this and declared it in Psalm 139:

> *O Lord, thou hast searched me and known me.*
> *Thou knowest my down sitting and my uprising;*
> *Thou understood my thought afar off.*
> *Thou compasseth my path and my*
> *Lying down, and art acquainted with all my ways.*
> *For there is not a word in my tongue, but lo,*
> *O Lord, thou knowest it.*
> *Thou had beset me behind and before.*
> *Where shall I go from thy Spirit?*
> *Or whether shall I flee from thy presence?*

God is the ever-present help in every circumstance .

GOD is ominipotent

He is all-powerful. There is no ammunition created by man or the devil that God cannot overcome if it is in his will to do so. No power can confront God's power. Pharaoh can testify to that

. Isaiah 54: 16-17 reads:

> *Behold I have created the smith that*
> *bloweth the coals in the fire, and that*
> *bringeth forth an instrument for his work;*
> *and I have created the waster to destroy.*

*No weapon that is formed against thee shall
prosper, and every tongue that shall rise
against thee in judgement, thou shall condemn
This is the heritage of the servant of the Lord
and their righteousness is of me saith
the Lord.*

We have the assurance of the presence of the Lord at all time. Everything out of his permission will not happen to his children. If he permits anything distasteful to his children anytime, know it, it is for rebuke, chastisement, training, discipline and growth.

GOD is **self- existing**
He does not depend on anyone to exist
Romans 11: 34-35 - Needs no counsel
.

GOD is **infinite**
Psalm 113:4,6. How can a finite man criticize the infinite God or question His activities? It is beyond man.

GOD is **jealous**
Exodus 20:5. He cannot share his glory with any being. Only Him alone must be worshiped and glorified.

Considering who God is, it is expedient for man to get acquainted with this only true, loving, forgiving, powerful, all- knowing, all -wise and ever- present God and to build a relationship with Him for His trustworthiness.

In this trouble-ridden world, one needs that God only to surrender to, and put absolute trust in, to have that peace that He alone can give.

This lead me to the strains and stresses that immigrant have to face in foreign land.

STRAINS AND STRESSES

The daily events of this present world deposit a lot of concern in the minds of individuals; troubling events may cause a sequence of trials in the physical, mental, emotional and spiritual realms of life. These worldly trials may result in anger, depression, anxiety and physical ailments like hypertension, insomnia, and alcohol dependency, to mention a few.

Many immigrants may be anxious about making ends meet financially. Some as a result of taking up two to three jobs thereby overstretch the physical body and strain the mind. The body is deprived of the essential rest it needs, becomes overworked and may start malfunctioning. Some immigrants permanently work day and night; this is against anybody's nature and can result in negative health.

This situation may have resulted from people who find themselves in jobs that are much below their education and below their living standard. In an attempt to improve their take-home pay, they get involved in too many jobs at the same time

; and they hope that whenever they update their qualification to suit the nation's requirement for better pay, they would relax ; in the meantime depression had set in and had resulted in extreme strains and stresses overwhelming them even before the better times arrive.

Health issues in a family can be a great concern for a breadwinner and the whole family as a whole. Many immigrants in the USA lack health insurance while immigrants in the UK lack adequate legal papers to earn them free health care under the social security system.

Loneliness, too, can be a big concern for an immigrant whose family may be thousands of miles away.

Job security is another factor that bothers most workers employed in foreign countries.

Accommodation problems are rampant among low-income immigrants. There is the issue of finding suitable housing; the issue of unfriendly neighbors, racial issues, admission of children to appropriate schools, and safety concerns for a family with children. There is also concern as to whether there will be suitable social activity that can facilitate relaxation as we know it in Africa, or the question of possible relocation to new environment and communities, . There is need for intimacy and confidentiality with fellow Africans, which will help make life more meaningful to Africans in a new country, a lack of which may result in depression or other health issues.

Another source of worry and concern for immigrants is the fact that loved ones left behind in the home country need attention. Bad health and lack of employment at home usually means that families left behind have to rely completely on their relative abroad. The relative may be unable to meet these family demands due to financial constraints and his personal problems.

There are other general issues like wars and rumors of war, terrorism, bad weather or some other mundane occurrences that worry the general public.

All other things may fade into insignificance compared with the spiritual battle that may face the individual. This may manifest in either the physical or in the spiritual dimension. This is a battle that can only be solved when one comes into relationship with the Prince of Peace.

All these situations enumerated above and many others that cannot be confined to this writing can cause strains and stresses that have got to be relieved for healthy and godly living.

There are many ailments that doctors cannot fully diagnose or cure. Many immigrants do not need medication but do need spiritual counseling. I know that doctors can be God's messengers to some curative process of certain conditions; therefore they definitely have their usefulness and thank God for them.

I can testify that there is no circumstance or condition that may affect man that there is no solution for. Solution can always be found in the book the Creator has published. This is the handbook or Instruction Manual for his creature - MAN. The book is the Bible. Man is the handiwork of God and if God's handbook is followed, the product man will perform well to the desired goal of the maker or manufacturer. If by chance the instruction is disregarded or ignored, man will not function rightly. If instruction is misread or misunderstood, help can be requested from the manufacturer on praying line. He promised to help those who need help.

Fortunately the maker is so generous and so caring over His creatures. He loves to communicate with those who trust Him as their Creator. If one is not acquainted with the Creator and is not on communicating terms with Him, there is no hope of proper functioning of the creature.

The Bible, God's manual for his creation has answers to all problems that confront man. It is the WORD of God. Jesus embodied the WORD.

John 1: 1-5 declares:
In the beginning was the WORD,
And the WORD was with God,
And the WORD was God.
The same was in the beginning with God.
All things were made by Him
Without him was not anything made that was made.
In him was life, and the life was the Light of men.
And the light shinneth in the darkness;
And the darkness comprehendeth it not.

Man cannot afford to ignore the instruction and guidance of the Creator without adverse result and unpalatable consequences.

At a time I was absolutely perplexed about a family problem and I could find no human solution to it. I thought the worst was definitely going to happen. Though I prayed, I probably worried more. At night in my sleep I heard that quiet distinct voice again saying, "Jesus is the solution to all problems." I woke up and thanked God. The problem did not get solved immediately but it got solved in God's way, when I turned it over to him. Praise God!

Psalm 46: 1 says,

God is our refuge and strength,
a very present help in trouble.

Psalm 121 confirms that help comes from the Lord, and that this Helper does not slumber nor sleep, He is capable for any situation and is never too busy to listen to prayer. He guides the going and coming of those who surrender to His guidance. He can attend to the whole world population at the same time because He is a spirit with divine personalities and attributes.

All that we are commanded to do to receive attention is to pray in Jesus name because He is the advocate for man. He never fails.

Some may think their situation has reached a stage where help is impossible.

Matthew 19:26 emphasises that:
With God all things are possible.

Mark 9:23

Everything is possible for him who believes.

There is nothing too difficult for God to do. He can open ways where there seems to be no way. He can create circumstances to effect his will for his obedient children. I can testify to this as well.

Some might think their type of illness cannot be cured. That is not according to God's word.

Jeremiah 30:17 declared,
For I will restore health unto thee
And I will heal thee of thy wounds
Saith the Lord.

1 Peter 2:24 talks about the healing capacity of our Savior.

With his own self bare our sins
In his own body on the tree, that we
Being dead to sins, should live unto
Righteousness; by whose stripes
Ye were healed.

Any disease can be healed if faith is exercised and doubt is not permitted and one focuses on Jesus Christ, the Healer.

In Isaiah 37 King Hezekiah prayed and was healed of his near-death ailment. He was given fifteen further years to live. There are many examples of spiritual healing in the Bible.

I personally have experienced spiritual healing even when doctors thought my condition was as a result of aging and that I had to live with it. I rejected that opinion and I decided to rely on my God alone with no help from any other person. Within a month, I was absolutely free from that ailment. I am writing this eighteen years later and I remain whole. Praise God.

God's favor in man's life can even turn enemies round and make them work for his benefit. I have testimonies to confirm this.
Romans 8:31 says,

If God be for us, who can be against us?

One may be worried and wondering what God will do about impending war or troublesome events in the world. Nothing happens that will take God by surprise. God is sovereign over all nations. We are to remain calm and pray knowing that God is in control and He cares for his own. All the miserable things happening in the world are caused by lack of love, mistrust, sinfulness, casting God aside, greed, and serving the gods of this world.

God is able to restore peace that passes all understanding in the hearts of believers.

Psalm 91 reads,
> *He that dwelleth in the secret place of*
> *The Most High shall abide under the shadow*
> *Of the Almighty.*
> *I will say of the Lord; He is my refuge and*
> *Fortress; my God; in him will I trust.*
> *Surely he shall deliver thee from the snare*
> *Of the fowler; and the noisome pestilence;*
>
> *He shall cover thee with his feathers,*
> *And under His wings shall thou trust;*
> *His truth shall be thy shield and buckler.*
> *Thou shalt not be afraid for the terror*
> *By night; nor for the arrows that flieth by day;*
> *Nor for the pestilence that walketh in darkness;*
> *Nor for the destruction that wasteth at noonday.*
> *A thousand shall fall at thy side, and*
> *Ten thousand at thy right hand, but it*
> *Shall not come near thee,… …,*

Readers are advised to read the whole psalm 91 to the end ..and believe in the unchanging words of God.,for he never fails.

The above psalm takes care of all types of weapons (biological , chemical, nuclear even spiritual) that may be fashioned against a child of God; such weapons will not prosper, as a matter of fact, they may backfire.

The Lord can make wars to seize; and he can make the enemies fight themselves as it has been read in the scriptures. It is all within his power.

The problem is that believers quite often allow fear and anxiety to dominate their lives. Fear is of the devil .

> God said in 2 Timothy 1:7:
> *For God hath not given us the spirit of fear,*
> *but of power, and of love, and of*
> *a sound mind*

Someone once said:" Worry is the interest paid on trouble before it comes due."

Shakespeare had earlier said, "Cowards die many times before their death."

> Billy Graham said,[3]
> If He cares for tiny birds and frail flowers,
>> why cannot we count on Him for our lives?
>> I know that modern living taxes the
> faith of the greatest Christians, but none of
>> us should doubt the ability of God to
> give us the grace sufficient for our trials

---

[3] Unto the Hills-A Daily Devotional - by Billy Graham on Answer to Anxiety.

even amid the stresses of this twentieth century. In the middle of our world troubles, the Christian is not to go about wringing his hands, shouting: "What shall we do?" having more nervous tensions and worry than anyone else. The Christian is to trust quietly that God is still on the throne. He is a sovereign God, working out things according to His own plan.

The fact that surpasses all our concern is that God loves us and cares about us. If we trust Him and remain under His protection, all things will work out to the glory of God and for our good. His Son, the Lord Jesus Christ is the Prince of Peace, as revealed in the Bible. If we search for peace through Christ, Christ himself promised to give that peace that surpasses all understanding to those who rely on Him.

This is well written in Songs of Praise written by J.C. Whittler 1807-92,[4]

Dear Lord and Father of mankind,
Forgive our fev'rish ways!
Reclothe us in our rightful mind;
In purer lives Thy service find,
In deeper rev'rence praise.

---

[4] Song of Praise. Hymn by John Greenleaf Whittier. 1807-92.

Felicia Oguntomilade

In simple trust like theirs who heard,
Beside the Syrian Sea,
Thy gracious calling of the Lord,
Let us, like them, without a word,
Rise up and follow Thee.

O Sabbath rest by Galilee!
O calm of hills above,
Where Jesus knelt to share with thee
The silence of eternity,
Interpreted by love.

Drop thy still dews of quietness,
Till all our strivings cease
Take from our souls, the strain and stress,
And let our ordered lives confess,
The beauty of thy peace.

Breathe through the heat of our desire,
Thy coolness and thy balm
Let sense be dumb, let flesh retire,
Speak through the earthquake, wind and fire,
O still small voice of calm!

That still small voice of calm is so soothing, so calm and so reassuring if believers hear it. Any believer can hear it if he communicates with God regularly. I have had this experience several times when nothing else could have achieved the purpose, but the voice did. God hears and listens to prayers. It is a sure line of communication with God and He replies in several ways if believers wait on Him and listen to Him too. Now, let readers focus on prayers and what can be achieved through prayers.

PRAYER

Now we know that God is our Creator. He is Omnipotent, Omnipresent and Omniscient. But that is not all; He loves his creation and loves to communicate with His creatures and He is interested in their welfare. What a God! What a privilege! He in His divine wisdom justifies believers, by amazingly giving his only begotten Son to die in their stead in order to redeem them. The same Son who is the same with the Father gave believers the assurance that if they ask His Father anything in His name Jesus, that He will answer them. It is only through Jesus that believers can find favor with God; through Him; believers have direct access to the source of all things. The same line of communication i.e. prayer, was practiced often by Jesus himself. When he was here with us physically on earth. Prayer was his life style..

Mark 1:35 records:
Very early in the morning, while it was still dark, Jesus got up, left the house and went

off to a solitary place, where he prayed.

Luke 6:12 records:
*Jesus went out into the hills to pray
and spent the night praying to God.*

He prayed anytime He wanted to heal,

He prayed at funerals, to raise the dead. He prayed over five loaves and two fishes, and these became sufficient to feed multitude, His fervent prayer at Gethsemane was recorded in all the gospels.

If the Son of God prays and showed us that it is the way to communicate with God, I wonder why any child of God will not take opportunity of this priceless process to reach the Almighty God.. He who is too occupied to pray is too busy to live a holy, abundant life in Christ.

Chrysostoma said,[5]

> The potency of prayer hath subdued the
> strength of fire, it hath bridled the
> rage of lions, hushed anarchy to rest,
> extinguished wars, expelled demons,
> burst the chains of death, expandeth
> the gates of heaven, assuaged
> diseases, repelled frauds,
> rescued cities from destruction,

---

[5] Quoted in a TREASURY OF PRAYER compiled by Leonard Ravenhill

stayed the sun in its course, and arrested
the progress of the thunderbolt.
Prayer is efficient panoply, a treasure
undiminished, a mine which is never
exhausted, a sky unobscured by clouds,
or heaven unruffled by storm.
It is the root, the fountain, and the mother
of a thousand blessings.

All these can be verified from the Bible. That same God who was God is still the same God today and will ever be God for ever and ever . Queen Mary of England was quoted to say that she feared the prayers of John Knox more than she feared all the armies of Scotland.

I have witnessed the testimonies of people who miraculously escaped their kidnappers' traps and dens just by calling on that precious name Jesus Christ. I have experienced God's answers to prayer in myriads of situations; enemies have become helpful despite themselves, finance has been made possible to meet special needs, child delivery had been safely procured in unusual ways, favor of God had been shown when needed, healing has been effected etc., etc. God remains faithful to his promises.

Psalm 34:15 says:
> *The Lord watches over the righteous*
> *And listens to their cries.*

Psalm 62:8 instructs:
> *Trust in God at all times my people,*

> *Tell him all your troubles for he is our*
> *Refuge.*

Isaiah 65:24 declares:
> *Before they call, I will answer, while they*
> *Are yet speaking, I will hear.*

Matthew 7:7 assures:
> Ask and it shall be given you,
>   seek and ye shall find,
>   knock and it shallbe open unto you.

James 4:12 warns:
> *Ye lust and have not, ye, kill and*
> *Desire to have , and cannot obtain*
> *Ye fight and war, yet ye have not*
> *Because ye ask not.*

The list of the efficiency of prayers is unlimited and so too are the number of people whose prayers have been answered in the Bible: Hezekiah, Jabez, Jacob, Isaac, Abraham, Paul, Silas, Enoch, Sarah, Elizabeth, Daniel etc., etc. These are people like any believer of these days, they were not super human, they only acted on their faith and knew whom they believed in ,and prayed to Him.

UNANSWERED PRAYERS

The Bible, the book of all wisdom gave reasons for prayers that seemed unanswered.

Hebrew 11:6 reads,
But without faith it is impossible to
please him; for he that cometh to God
must believe that he is , and that he is a
rewarder of them that diligently
seek him

When we pray we need to have faith in who we praying to, otherwise we should not expect an answer.

As humans if we want something from our human father, and our mind and action portrays doubt in his fatherhood and his ability to provide the requests, that father will not feel obliged to respond.

James 1:5-8 catigorically says
If any of you lack wisdom, let him ask
Of God, that giveth to all men liberally,
And upbreadeth not; and it shall be given
Him. But let him ask in faith, nothing
Wavering. For he that wavereth is like
A wave in the sea, driven with the wind
And tossed. For let not that man think he
Shall receive from the Lord.
A double minded man is unstable in
All his ways.

Some people doubt when they pray because they think that their request is too big or that God cannot answer that type of request. God is concerned with every aspect of believers' lives; nothing is too small or too big or too mundane for him to attend to..

Other people think they are not holy enough for God to consider them. None of his creature is good enough for the Holy God. He knew mankind in their desperation and that is why His Son has come to pay for our sins. By the imputation of believers' sin on Jesus and reciprocally the imputation of Christ's righteousness on believers , God sees believers as righteous, justified ,discharged and acquited from all iniquities. Without the vicarious atoning blood of Jesus on the cross of calvary, there would have been no hope for mankind.

> Isaiah 64:6
> *But we are all as an unclean thing; and*
> *All our righteousness are as filthy rags.*

David the great king of Israel was a man like we are, he committed sins just as we do, but he learnt to confess his sins to God and to plead for mercy. He knew God enough to fear him and love him and ask for forgiveness as he did in Psalm 51, which is an example for all sinners for confessing and turning away from sins

David knew that God could wash him clean as white as snow. He asked for a clean heart and renewal of a right spirit within him, a thorough rebirth, a complete regeneration . This is what all believers need. The blood of Jesus cleanses us from all our uncleanness.

When man accepts Jesus Christ as his Savior he is said to be 'born again' with a new spirit being born in him. He is a new baby in the Spirit and has to grow. As he is yielding to the leading of the indwelling Spirit, he continues to mature in the knowledge and way of Christ passing through teething, toddler, and adolescence stages and maturing gradually to reach the goal Christ has set for an active believer. Every believer passes through this process and there is no perfection in any man until the second coming of our Lord Jesus. We only deceive ourselves when we say we have no sin. Like the prodigal son, there is a father waiting for the sinner to come home.

The Lord's Prayer is the very example of prayer given to us in Matthew 6:9; the Lord taught the disciples to ask for forgiveness of sins as they forgive others that trespass against them. This is a condition that believers must incline their hearts to keep in order to be forgiven. Many hold grudges, malice and vengeance in their hearts. This is blocking the path of God for hearkening unto their prayers. The parable of Jesus about the two debtors in Matthew 18: 23-34 tells about the unforgiving servant. When he was forgiven his big debt and set free, he chose not to forgive another man who owed him a little. He decided to fully punish his fellow man. His own master showed him how wicked he was and he got the punishment he deserved.

Another impediment to prayer is asking amiss. James 4:3 reads:

*Ye ask and receive not, because ye
ask amiss, that ye may consume it upon
your lust and mis use what God may have graciously
given you !.*

When a married man goes out of his home to entice another man's wife for her beauty or for whatever reason; he then prays that he will not be caught or that the judge will acquit him of his lust. A just God will not hearken unto this type of prayer.

Proverbs 6: 27-29 reads:
*Can a man take fire in his bosom
And his clothes not be burned?
Can one go upon hot coals and his
Feet not be burned?
So he that goeth into his neighbors wife
Whosoever toucheth her shall not go innocent.*

Sometimes a man may ask for wrong things that God knows will not be beneficial to him, or that is not God-honoring.

In Matthew 7: 9-11 Jesus said
*Which of you, if his son ask for
Bread, will give him a stone? Or if he ask*

*For a fish will give him a snake? If
You who are evil, know how to give good gifts
To your children, how much more will your
Father in heaven give good gifts to those
Who ask him!*

In that sense also, if a person ask for snake, the Lord will not grant him because it will not be good for him.

HOW TO PRAY

Prayer is just communication with heavenly Father. It is very simple as taught by the Lord Jesus Christ in Matthew 6: 9-13:

*Our Father which art in heaven
Hallowed be thy name
Thy Kingdom come
Thy will be done on in earth, as it is in heaven.
Give us this day our daily bread
And forgive us our debts, as we forgive
our debtors.
And lead us not into temptation, but deliver
us from evil; For thine is the kingdom, and
the power, and the glory, forever. Amen.*

This is a pattern to guide believers in their prayer. Simply translated, it is to acknowledge who God is and worship him;

to thank him for sustenance and benefits received. Confess any known sin and ask for pardon. Harbor no grudges i.e. forgive others who might have wronged you. Make your request known to God in the name of Jesus. Ask for guidance and direction so that Satan will not take control. Thank God believing that you will receive what you asked for. Worship him for his authority and power. Be very sincere.

HOW OFTEN TO PRAY

Being a Christian is having relationship with the divine heavenly Father through His son Jesus Christ. In Africa, when a child wakes up in the morning, he reverently and lovingly greets his earthly parents. It is believed that this attitude brings a response of blessings to the child from the parents. This same custom is repeated in the evening or night before he retires to sleep. When he goes out daily for his duties or jobs, there is also an exchange of greeting as well as when he returns. Parents are gratefully thanked when they give gifts and they are affectionately loved and respected for being who they are. This is relationship.

It is exactly the same with our heavenly Father. Most people find time in the morning to pray ie to commune with God. It is very necessary. If time allows, (and that time should be made) it is good to spend about ten minutes communing with the Lord; thanking Him for enabling one to see a new day, and asking Him to lead one through this new day's activities. After the day's job, a believer should build a good habit of reporting back to the One who led you on.successfully

Prayer is not limited to those morning and nighttime periods only. The Bible teaches us to pray without ceasing. This means that during the course of the day or night, every thought and activity must be surrendered to God without drawing attention to any one. You do not need to kneel down or ncessarily cry out at such times. It is a quiet prayer relying on God in all circumstances, the one God who hears one in quietness will respond assuredly. Constantly practiced, silent prayer becomes a part of one; one considers same as a walk with God at any time, on the road, in the office, in the kitchen, in the nursery, before interviews and in all circumstances. God is always listening, and God will always respond as necessary for His will and for His glory

ANSWERS TO PRAYERS

God who knows the intention of the heart surely knows the prayers one offers unto him. When what is prayed for is obtained, one feels that the prayer has been answered. Our earthly fathers sometimes say "yes" or "no" to our requests. The concept is the same, except that the earthly father may say 'no' when he cannot fulfill our requests. The heavenly Father has unlimited resources to grant everybody's requests but He knows that certain requests will not be beneficial to one. His answer to a request may be 'No' because it is not good, or it will not be the best or of lasting interest for the purpose that God has for that person. His answer may be 'Wait' because the time is not ripe for the person to appreciate such a request. God knows us more than we know ourselves. He knows the outcome of things before the beginning and so he is in the best position to make a beneficial decision to any request made to him.

When one gets more intimate with communion with God, one will learn, as a believer, how to understand God's response in trust and with gratitude, knowing that He loves and wants the best for his children in order to reach the goal He set for them. It is a wonderful, satisfying, loving relationship that is divine; this relationship will mean everything to a maturing Christian and helps to improve relationships among fellow men and women.

Human tragedies happen occasionally, but not because God does not hear us or has stopped loving. It is part of life in the world to have to face such things, but God sees us through and comforts us. At times through the difficulty, God makes a way for the believer to grow and shine forth for God's purpose. This takes me to a song written by someone who experienced the friendship of Jesus through a personal tragedy of the loss of his fiancée just before marriage.:

WHAT A FRIEND WE HAVE IN JESUS[6]

What a friend we have in Jesus
All our sins and griefs to bear!
What a privilege to carry
Everything to God in prayer!

O what peace we often forfeit
O what a needless pain we bear
All because we do not carry
Everything to God in prayer.

Have we trials and temptations?
Is there trouble anywhere?
We should never be discouraged
Take it to the Lord in prayer

Can we find a friend so faithful
Who will all our sorrows share
Jesus knows our every weakness
Take it to the Lord in prayer.

Are we weak and heavy laden
Cumbered with a load of care?
Precious Savior, still our refuge
Take it to the Lord in prayer.

---

[6] Joseph M. Shriven Hymn book

Felicia Oguntomilade

> *Do the friends despise, forsake thee?*
> *Take it to the Lord in prayer*
> *In His arms He'll take and shield thee*
> *Thou wilt find a solace there.*
> by Joseph Medicott Shriven
>   1819-1886

I like this serenity prayer that I came across in a devotional book.[7]

> *God grant me the serenity to accept things*
> *that I cannot change, the courage to*
> *change the things I can, and wisdom*
> *to know the difference.*

PRACTICAL HELP TO PRAYER

PERSISTENCE

When there is a definite need either for self or for another person, and you are asking in good faith, one does not give up readily on your asking. This is reflected in the parable of Jesus in Luke 11:5-8.

> *Which one of you shall have a friend,*
> *and shall go into him by midnight, and*
> *say unto him, Friend lend me three loaves,*
> *For a friend of mine in his journey is come*
> *to me, and I have nothing to set before him.*

---

[7] Serenity Prayer - Devotional book.

And he from within shall answer and say,
Trouble me not: the door is now shut: and
my children are with me in bed, I cannot
Rise and give thee I say unto you,
though he will not rise and give him
because he is his friend,
yet because of his importunity, he will
rise and give him as many as he needeth.

Jesus cares for believer's need and ready to meet him at the point of his need.

One does not give up on prayer because a request has not been granted the first time. One remains persistent like the Canaanite woman who asked Jesus to heal her sick daughter. Jesus first teasingly tried her faith, being a Canaanite and not of Israel belief. She persisted, saying in Matthew 15: 21-28:

Truth Lord; yet the dogs eat of
the crumbs which fall from their
master's table.

She humbly received the healing and Jesus remarked on her great faith. It took faith, humility and persistence. She knew that Jesus could heal her daughter.

DISCIPLINE

There are times when there is a need to subdue the body through fasting and concentrating on requests for a period of time. Fasting is a private activity and should not be for public showing.. It depresses flesh to attune the spirit to divine line and makes communication easier, definite and purposeful. Jesus advocated this especially by example of his fasting for forty days and forty nights in the wilderness. Moses and Elijah were recorded as fasting and many other great spiritualists fast for concentration and purposeful prayers. Consequently, they achieved great things for the kingdom.

GODLY LIVING
Romans 6: 1,2

> *What shall we say then? Shall we continue in sin, that grace may abound? God forbid. How shall we that are dead to sin, be any longer therein*
>
> .

This is a call to holy living. It is by grace that believers are saved and that grace must not be abused. God cannot be mocked. Believers are not perfect, but as much as they can humanly try, and with the help of Him that lives within them, they should try to be godly in their daily living so that their prayers will not be hindered. Romans chapter 12 is recommended for reference in godly living.

HOPE AND FAITH
Hebrews 11:1 reads

> *Now Faith is the substance of things*

hoped for, the evidence of things not seen.

Faith is the bedrock of prayer. Without faith, there is no point in praying. One should be very hopeful, ready to receive, not doubting when you pray. One should believe that one will obtain what one is seeking for. One should be very persistent and very positive like the Canaanite woman or like blind Barthemeus, or the woman with the issue of blood. They were rewarded with what they confidently expected that they would get from Jesus.

AVOID NEGATIVITY

Some new immigrants are made to feel they are different. It might be because they are of different color, or because they are not educated enough, or because their accent is different, or because of any other type of negativity the world system may wrap them with. They should know what God thinks about them and his love for them. Each immigrant may be different but each immigrant is unique. Each should exhibit that confidence and pray and press on with one's goal, asking God for unusual favor which He alone can give. The immigrant may be pleasantly surprised and uniquely rewarded,,for His purpose will ripen faster than people around can imagine. With God all things are possible.

BE THANKFUL

One should make one's request known to God with thanks. And remember to thank God always for benefits received every day. One's blessings should be routinely counted and be thankful. God will not share his glory with any man, give glory to God and praise him always.

At the conclusion of this chapter, we reiterate that help comes from the Lord. He is ready and willing to help those who surrender to and trust in him. If a reader does not already belong to a church, he should find a Bible- believing vibrant church where he or she can fellowship. One should not merely remain a bench warmer but be very proactive with the work of the kingdom.

Remember if God is with one, who can be against the one?

PRAYER

Father God, in the name of your eternal Son Jesus Christ, I thank you for your great love for me. I appreciate the value you put on me by sending your son to the cross for me. Pardon my ignorance of how unique and purposeful you have made me. Help me to understand my worth through your eyes and be grateful. Lord, give me spiritual ears to hear from you and listen to your guidance in my life. I now know you are a very present help in my situation. (May mention your special request.) I pray for your favor to follow me in all my ways. Make thy way plain before my eyes as you lead me on. Give me the peace and security that passes all understanding. I give you all the glory and honor and praise in Jesus name. Amen.

5

CONFLICTING CULTURES

To a very large extent, communities that share a common knowledge, a common belief, a common memory: that allow the people to communicate reasonably and live together harmoniously are believed to belong to the same cultural heritage. In many instances, these values and ideas dictate their mode of dressing, their character, their eating habits and their relationships.

In this age and time when the whole world has become a global village, the world has become a fertile ground of cultural mixing bowl, for ideas travel through the internet, radio, and television at an alarming rate. If you sneeze in London this minute, America has known about it, China is taking note and Africa is not ignorant about it. The speed of communication thus affects ways of life in every corner of the globe. Unfortunately, this does not translate to a universal culture in which we all understand one another, or behave alike and live harmoniously by sharing the same idea and pursuing the same goals. On a fortunate note however, had one universal culture been created, it would have resulted from some ungodly cultural practices and behaviors having been enforced on all individual communities in the world by the more influential and the more advanced communities.

A cultural identity can probably be contained without migration of different people to different places as we now have all over the world.

A perfect example of conflicting cultures can be read in the Bible, how the Israelites could not readily mix with the Egyptians despite the governor status of Joseph. The Egyptians refused to fully accept the Israelites too. The Israelites lived in Goshen and did things their own way which eventually led to the exodus and the parting of ways. Their values, goals and ways of life were far apart despite the fact that human basic needs for shelter, food, clothing and security were the same. The truth is that a stronger community will always want to lord it over a weaker community either for fear of losing their strong hold or because they are prejudiced.

Sometimes the line between cultural misunderstanding and actual assault is difficult to determine as an immigrant. In 1994 a Filipino immigrant couple living in San Francisco Bay lost custody of their five offspring over accusation of sexual abuse of the children by their paternal grandmother and an uncle. According to the Filipino News, the grandmother may have spoken of the children's private parts in jest and even touched them when she was bathing them. The Department of Social Services interpreted this as abuse. The Department told the immigrant couple that they could only regain the custody of their children if they admitted that an abuse had indeed occurred. The thirty year old father who was a maintenance operator at an area high school was faced with a hard choice.

[8] "My wife is home everyday, but she had not seen anything wrong.....and if I do say that I believe the children, even if it were true, he added, what would happen to my mother? They will put her in jail."

This example and many other practices that are viewed innocent by different cultures, but not by the culture of the countries of immigration, are embarrassing and confusing. It is therefore essential for any immigrant to be culturally educated in his present state of settlement.

Immigrants should also endeavor to educate their relatives, especially the older ones, to avoid practices that are not acceptable where they live. Children must be encouraged to talk to their parents first before ever talking to outsiders about their grievances; and parents must listen to their children and be proactive at home to avoid embarrassment and collision with the law.

---

[8] Manuel Barros, 1995 A1b

Culturally sensitive clinicians believe that behavior deemed acceptable in third world countries can sometimes be erroneously labeled as child abuse, or wife abuse or relative abuse depending on the circumstances, e.g. co-sleeping with siblings, which to individual immigrant, is either being supportive or is a necessity due to space shortage, and which has nothing to do with sexual motive, can be misinterpreted by social officers of first world countries. It is also learnt that the "Constant teasing about genitals" which pre-adolescent boys endure in the Philippians is deemed improper within the American culture.. [9] Perhaps many African immigrants may be confronted with similar challenging situations in their families, personal relationships, work relationships and amongst acquaintances..

It is advised that African immigrants should be aware that certain foreign "practices and values" may be intolerable to others. To be culturally literate in a new environment may call for cultural adjustment for one's peace of mind, mutual respect, social acceptability and the avoidance of sensational embarrassing news.

Laws are instituted to protect the poor and the weak; and also establish the rights of citizens, always emphasizing that the right of one is limited by the right of the .other.

,The question of "right" or "wrong" has been appreciated in many cultures, but it has been respectively rated relevant to each ethnic, traditional, faith-based background of

---

[9] YAP, 1986: 131-132

each community. When one therefore chooses to leave one's community to live in another community, logically it is for one's peace and the peace of others to obey the law of the new community; this is what freedom is all about.

Freedom is paramount in the heart of human beings; freedom to learn, to trade, to practice one's faith, freedom to speak and freedom to reach a desired goal without persecution or prejudice.

Any where in the world where these basic freedom desires are attainable, there must be laws to protect such freedom or else, one person's freedom may become a disadvantage or nuisance to another person ,for one person's right must be limited by the right of another person. This is why democracy is the fairest form of government next to Theocracy. It is a system of government in which power is vested in the people who rule either directly or through freely elected representatives. Democracy will be better still when the rulers know and fear the real God of creation whose love for mankind is so intense that he has planned our true freedom by giving us His eternal beloved son to save us from sin and enslavement of sin, now and till eternity.

All the myriads of laws of governments in the universe are derived, with modifications, from God's laws given to Moses on Mount Sinai. The presentation of these laws in different countries depends on the interpretation in the minds of the rulers to suit their communities or protect their egos, or to defend their religion. I believe that the best culture can be found in God's laws, which reveal who He is, and what He thinks is good and beneficial for mankind whom He created in His wisdom. Human evolving cultures vary from country to country, according to their priorities, wisdom and values with the ultimate purpose of what they consider peaceful . God's laws remain constant in His Omniscience and He is the author of peace and concord.

His prescription for our behavior and way of life is the solution to all problems we face on this planet earth. The Laws of God as given as the decalogue in Exodus 20: 3-17:

1. *Thou shall have no other gods before me.*
2. *Thou shall not make unto thee any graven image, or any likeness of anything that is in heaven above, or in the earth beneath, or that is in the water under the earth. Thou shall not bow down thyself to them, nor serve them, for I the Lord thy God am a jealous God, visiting the iniquity of the fathers upon the children unto the third and forth generation of them that hate me. And shewing mercy unto thousands of them that love me and keep my commandments.*
3. *Thou shall not take the name of the Lord thy God in vain; for the Lord will not hold him guiltless that taketh His name in vain.*
4. *Remember the Sabbath day, to keep it holy. Six days shalt thou labor, and do all thy work .But the seventh day is the sabbath of the Lord thy God; in it, thou shall not do an y work, thou, nor thy son, nor*

thy daughter, nor thy man servant, nor thy cattle, nor thy stranger that is within thy gates;For in six days the Lord made heaven and earth, the sea, and all that in them is, and rested the seventh day; wherefore the Lord blessed the Sabbath day and hallowed it.

5. *Honor thy father and thy mother; that thy days may be long upon the land which the Lord thy God giveth thee.*
6. *Thou shalt not kill.*
7. *Thou shalt not commit adultery.*
8. *Thou shalt not steal.*
9. *Thou shalt not bear false witness against thy neighbor.*
10. *Thou shalt not covet thy neighbor's wife, nor his man servant, nor his maid servant, nor his ox, nor his ass, nor anything that is thy neighbors.*

These laws or commandments should govern our moral life. Immorality is the bane of most societies in this age and thus results in various diseases, moral confusion, divorces, sexual atrocities, and perversions. The display of sex in every sphere of society, the marketing of sex on television, Internet and radio, billboard, sports and in almost every medium, gives the impression of acceptance and no remorse.

God's laws and commandments should also govern our social life. These laws tell us how to maintain and sustain our relationship with others. They instruct us on property rights and labor responsibilities and respect for others. The laws also take into consideration our needed relaxation and rest and most importantly the recognition of our maker.

The laws govern our relationship with this maker. Absence of this recognition and failure to worship makes life meaningless, purposeless, boring and leads to destruction here on earth and definitely in eternity.

Billy Graham said in one of his soul winning crusades,[10]

> Life with Christ is endless love,
> without Christ is a loveless end.

It does not matter how long we live on earth, it is an infinitestimal fraction of time in eternity; but how we live and the choice we make of our faith; determines where we spend our eternity. There is no room for people to stand on the fence; the choice is either hell or heaven, the Lake of fire burning with brimstone or the New City Jerusalem !!!.

God is interested in our governance hence we are told in 1 Timothy 2:

> *I exhort therefore that first of all,*
> *supplication, prayers, intercession and*
> *giving of thanks be made for all men.*
> *For kings, and for all that are in authority:*

---

[10] Crusade Speech by Billy Graham

*that ye may lead a quiet and peaceable life
in all godliness and honesty.*

People in authority make rules and regulations that control the lives of citizens. They also have authority to punish offenders. The Bible teaches that the rulers do not bear the rod in vain - and that they are God's servants for judgment and praise. This is why we should choose God-fearing rulers and sustain rulers with prayer so that they will rule with the fear of God, seeking justice for all, and peace for their citizens. The fact remains that all human efforts for peace without the "Prince of Peace" is futile.

A sum up of God's laws can be found in the discussion between Jesus and the Pharisee who was a lawyer. The smart tempting lawyer asked Jesus, saying in Matthew 22: 36-40:

*Master, which is the great commandment in the law?
Jesus said unto him, Thou shalt love the Lord
thy God with all thy soul and with all thy mind.
This is the first and great commandment.
And the second is like unto it. Thou
shalt love thy neighbor as thyself.
On these two commandments hang
all the law and the prophets.*

All our modern laws can be traced back to these two commandments. There is no separation of law and state in a Christian life. We live in love and reverential fear of the Lord and love and respect our neighbors as ourselves. If we do not then we should. God is interested in all His creatures and is not partial and is no "respecter" of person.

This can be seen in the life of Abraham and Sarah, Ishmael and his mother. God cared for Ishmael and his mother even in the desert, though he had plans for Isaac as the promised son. The result of that saga which was caused by human failing on both sides is the source of world disturbance up to this day. God cares for our rights in Him and has an eternal master plan for humanity. HISTORY IS HIS STORY.

In concluding this chapter, "God's" culture as seen in his laws superimposes all human culture on planet earth. It is essential to obey the law of the land where you reside so that you may live in peace. The root of these various laws is to fear God and love your neighbor as yourself. Man must recognize that there is a supreme God who loves all his creatures and who is the author of peace and concord. He is a righteous One and is sovereign over all nations as recorded in Psalm 47:2. Whether those nations recognize the fact or not, God's purpose will be fulfilled, no human effort can forestall it. More than anything else is the fact that Jesus is the fulfillment of all the laws. In him only, we can take refuge.

PRAYER

Father God, I thank you for who you are. You are my creator, my savior, and my love. I give glory to you for your greatness and awesomeness. It is so reassuring that you are sovereign over all the nations and that you care for me. I pray

Lord, for your wisdom and discretion to guide me in my work and my relationship with others. I know that you can perfect all that concerns me; therefore I rest my situation under your loving control.

Keep me Lord, close to you because I need you all the time. Help me Lord to keep thy laws by the power of your Holy Spirit dwelling in me. Let my life reflect your purpose for me and be an example for others to emulate in Jesus Name Amen.

6

AFRICANS CAN INFLUENCE OTHERS IN GODLY VALUES

There is no race that can lay claim to perfection over other races; every race is in a process of improving itself. This process continues as long as we live. The goal of every individual group or person depends on whom they accept as their guru, or champion or hero. For the Christian of any race, the Master, the Mentor is the Savior, the Lord Jesus Christ who was the perfect man and He is Lord!

African immigrants should examine the values they hold fast; those values that are godly, those that honor God and those that are of benefit to others. These values can be revived in individual families or communities. They cannot be enforced on other people but, as they are lived by, and practiced, these values will be admired and may be copied. Actions, as the saying goes, speak louder than words. This is what Paul was saying to the Corinthians in 2 Corinthians 3:2:

Ye are our epistle written in our
hearts and read of all men.

If every aspect of an immigrant life reflects the goodness of Jesus Christ, that life-style will not be hidden and it will be of benefit to others. Some may criticize, some may think it is old fashioned or foolish compared with the ways of the world, but others will admire and emulate good ideas. The immigrant who endeavors to live a godly life will have inner satisfaction and the peace of God and peace with God whether people like it or not.

Love of Family

Most Africans base their values on their family. They live to honor their family and to win prestige for their community. Any disgraceful act tends to reflect on the family and so it is avoided so as not to attach the stigma to that generation. This is one of the major reasons why children are brought up properly and disciplined appropriately and nurtured lovingly.

In many African societies, this nurturing is usually done by grandparents who combine nurturing with story telling (stories with moral and ethical flavor) and narrative history of ancestors to boost the morality and energy of their children and grandchildren. The fact that some have migrated is not an excuse to deprive children of this valuable education. Children get interested and ask questions from their grandparents which they cannot ask their immediate parents. The parents of these immigrant children owe it to their children to prevent other cultures being forced upon them if they are not equipped with their own. Some of these other cultures may be detrimental to their health and morals. America, for example is a multi-cultural society, and if the children have nothing to own and be proud of, they are gravitated to other undesirable practices by their peers before the parents become aware of it and try to correct it. No matter how busy parents are, they must find time to speak to their children and instill values in them.

The Bible instructs us to train our children

Proverbs 22:6 :
> *Train up a child in the way he should go;*
> *and when he is old he will not depart from it.*

Proverbs 13:20:
> *He who spares the rod hates his son*
> *but he who loves him is careful to discipline him.*

This is not an excuse to abuse ones child. There are so many ways a child can be disciplined in love and not in bitterness. Every child needs discipline otherwise the parents will regret the outcome of lack of discipline in a child that grows in this permissive era and generation.

In Africa when children are born, parents and grandparents give meaningful names to their newborn. A name may reflect the wish of the parents for the child, or reflect the circumstances surrounding the birth of the child, or a name may reflect how the child was born, it may reflect the heroes of the family, or even the faith of the family.

These names whether considered or not, do influence the child's aspirations and character and many times can dictate the goal of life for that child. A prime example of meaningful naming of a child can be found in the Bible. Matthew 1:20-21

> *But while he thought of these things,*
> *Behold the angel of the Lord*
> *Appeared unto him in a dream,*
> *Saying, Joseph, thou son of David,*
> *Fear not to take unto thee Mary thy wife;*
> *For that which is conceived in her is of*
> *The Holy Ghost. And she shall bring forth*
> *A son, and thou shall call his name Jesus!*
> *For he shall save his people*
> *From their sins.*

The angel Gabriel revealed the purpose of God sending his son to earth by naming him accordingly. This is a divine example of naming a child purposely. Another example is found in 1 Samuel 1:20:

> *Wherefore it came to pass when the time*
> *was come about after Hannah had conceived,*

> *that she bore a son, and call his name Samuel,*
> *saying, Because I have asked him of the Lord.*

"Samuel "means God has heard. That is the reason for naming him.

Another example in 1Samuel 25:20:
> *Let not my Lord, I pray thee regard*
> *this man of Balial, even Nabal, for as*
> *His name is: is he - Nabal is his name,*
> *and folly is with him.*

This was the answer of a wise Abigail to David, when the husband Nabal acted foolishly towards David by refusing to help David and his troops. David and his men had earlier helped to protect Nabal's flock in the field, and one good turn should deserve another. Abigail said this to protect the husband and their household, otherwise David and his army would have retaliated. In this narrative, Nabal acted as his name implied - Foolish.

These are just a few of several examples in the Bible where names are given to reveal the historical events surrounding the birth, the wish of parents for the child, the prayer of parents and their hopes for their children. Africans absolutely agree with these examples.

Africans love their children and they wish and want the best for them. A naming ceremony is elaborately done because of its importance; it is like giving direction to the life of that child and planting the child firmly into the family roots.

Children that are born alive are given names like examples below:

Babafemi or Oluwafemi	-God loves me (Nigeria)
Ezeamaka	-King or kingship is splendid or good (Nigeria)
Chidi or Olurun-nimbe	-God exists (Nigeria)
Nassor	-Victorious (Tanzania)
Muwai	-Good fortune (Malawi)
Gamba	-Warrior (Zimbabwe)
Osei	-Noble (Ghana)
Simba	-Lion (Botswana) denoting strength
Sipho	-Gift (South Africa)
Oluwasegun	-The Lord has given victory (Nigeria)
Afam	-Friendly (Ghana)
Alaezi	-I am exonerated (Nigeria)
Oluwadare	-I am justified (Nigeria)
Chinyere	-God is the giver (Nigeria)
Oluwaseyi	-The Lord is the giver (Nigeria)

Halima	-Gentle (East Africa)
Modupe	-I am grateful (Nigeria)
Kikelomo	-A child to be loved and cherished (Nigeria)
Omolere	-A child is a blessing (Nigeria)
Taiwo	-1st of twins (Nigeria)
Kehinde	-2nd of twins (Nigeria)
Nataki	-Of high birth (East Africa)
Shanifa	-Sunshine (Somalia)
Danladi	-Born on Saturday (Nigeria)
Bosede	-Born on Sunday (Nigeria)
Ekundayo	-Sorrow has turned to happiness (Nigeria)
Kamau	-Quiet warrior (Kenya)
Oluyemisi	-God has honored me (Nigeria)
Olumayowa:	-The Lord has brought us joy (Nigeria)

These are just samples of names that reflect African custom. This tradition should continue for posterity and for the good of the children. People of other cultures or Africans that have lost touch with home may copy this custom for their own pleasure and good of the children who will reflect and respond back to their names. These names should be thoughtfully and prayerfully given as done in Africa.

Abortion is not a welcome or accepted practice in Africa - it is foreign. It appears to be tolerated by some First World countries for convenience and for seeming lack of fear of God. It is ungodly and Christians should avoid the practice. It is better to be disciplined in sex life than to revel in reckless uncontrolled sex life and subsequently commit murder. It is not civilized to commit murder. It is barbaric.

RESPECT OF ELDERS

Africans in general have great respect and regard for elders. In rural areas, all aged people are addressed Papa or Mama or any accolade used for personal father or mother. People generally look up to elders for wisdom and direction.

The Bible, which is God's plan and direction and wisdom for believers, has a lot to say about elders

1 Peter 5:5:
> *Likewise ye younger, submit yourselves unto the elder: yea all of you be subject to one another, and be clothed with humility, for God resisted the proud, and giveth grace to the humble.*

Leviticus 19:32:

> *Thou shalt rise up before the hoary*
> *head, and honor the face of the old man;*
> *and fear thy God: I am the Lord.*

Job 32:6
> *And Elihu the son of Barachel the*
> *Buzite answered and said: I am young*
> *and ye are very old; wherefore I was*
> *afraid and didst not shew you my opinion.*

Proverbs 23:22
> *Hearken unto thy father that begat thee*
> *and despise not thy mother when she is old.*

1 Timothy 5:1-2
> *Rebuke not an elder, but entreat him*
> *as a father, and the younger one*
> *as brother.*

Exodus 20:12 stipulates
> *Honor thy father and thy mother:*
> *that thy days may be long upon the*
> *land which thy Lord thy God giveth thee.*

Any African will favorably identify with the word of God on relationship with elders. No amount of civilization can nullify the word of God; and the fact that African culture is built on reverence and identification of elders. Children born or nurtured outside Africa should be made to appreciate this part of our culture and must be not allowed to copy irreverent culture. There is nothing uncivilized or slavish by any person answering 'Sir' or 'Ma'am' to their elders; as a matter of fact, the act shows that the person has proper upbringing. Others, who at first may want to look down on a person showing respect, will eventually emulate the person when they realize that it is a sign of good manners.

Children or young people can always give a cultured reply to elders instead of 'talking back' to them, when seemingly provoked.

Actions speak louder than words; negative body language or certain negative action when directed towards elders, can bring out a reaction of shock, insult or embarrassment, unknown to the culprit, who might have been brought up outside their parent's culture. This is not necessarily the fault of these youngsters; but a lack of parental influence over the surrounding culture. It is not easy to emulate the African culture in non-African environment, but it can be achieved by example, by living close to fellow Africans and by the word of God in teaching the children. Schools cannot impart African values into our children; it has to start from home.

First name calling is disrespectful to elders in African culture. Elderly people can be addressed "Mr., Mrs., or Miss' before their names. This manner of addressing elders was the cultured attitude in European civilization some fifty years ago. Some still adhere to it, but to many, it is old fashioned and not 'cool'. The word of God is not affected by age and time. What was good then, remains good now.

Africans do not need to copy everything the Western culture has to offer especially if it is contrary to the word of God and offensive to Africans. There are African values with moral philosophy to fall back on; and the word of God will give the spiritual backing and strength to live by them.

Considering the opinion of elders on certain issues is an act of respect and is scriptural. 1 King 12 tells how Rehoboam the King of Israel shunned the opinion of elders who served and advised his father Solomon well; rather he took to the opinion of his young reckless advisers which led to the division of his kingdom.

1 King 12: 6-8

The King Rehoboam consulted the elders
who has served his father Solomon in his lifetime:
"How would you advise me to answer the people?"
he asked.

They replied, "if today you will be a servant
to these people and serve them and give
them a favorable answer, they will
always be your servant.

But Rehoboam rejected the advice the
elders gave him and consulted the young men

*who had grown up with him. He asked them,
"What is you advice? How should we answer
these people who say to me "Lighten the yoke
your father put on us."
The young men replied;*

*"Tell them, my little finger is thicker
than my fathers waist. My father laid
on you a heavy yoke; I will make it heavier.
My father scourged you with whips; I will
scourge you with scorpions."*

The result was the division of the kingdom whereby Rehoboam held on to two tribes, the greater part (10 tribes), was ruled by another king. It became a weakened divided kingdom; the Northern Kingdom was taken into captivity by the Assyrians in 721 BC whilst the Southern Kingdom was taken into captivity by the Babylonians in 586 BC.

Moses honored the advice Jethro gave him in Exodus 18. It helped him in the administration of Israel under God in the wilderness. Through the advice, Moses delegated authority to some elders so that he could concentrate on more important issues of the kingdom under God.

These are examples of how elders have their position of authority and also possess wisdom in years, attributes that can guide younger people to better their lives.

Felicia Oguntomilade
DRESSING

Dressing is a practice and activity all over the world to cover a man or woman's nakedness. When our first parents Adam and Eve discovered they were naked after disobeying God and obeying Satan, despite God's instruction not to eat a particular fruit, they attempted to cover up with fig leaves (Genesis 3). Still, though they succeeded in covering their physical bodies, they were spiritually naked. God himself assisted them, making it possible for Adam and Eve to cover their physical bodies with garments made out of skin of animals; in other words God had killed an animal and shed its blood on behalf of Adam and Eve,thus perhaps atoning for their sins ,a pointer to the eventual "cover" for man's spiritual nakedness 'sin',which will be the full and final sacrifice of the sinless Son of God on Calvary for the penalty of man's sin. The only way a sinful man can return to God is by the grace of the ransom paid by Jesus Christ, God's Son.

Dressing is done principally to cover the physical body. In Deuteronomy 22:5 the word of God says:

A woman must not wear men's
clothing, nor a man wear women's
clothing for the Lord your God
detests anyone who does this.

African Immigrants

The reason is clear. It is intended to prohibit such perversion as transvestitism and homosexuality. God created differences between men and women, and any attempt to blur these differences is a cause of confusion and an excuse for perversion. A woman should remain feminine and graceful in her dressing. Obscenity in dressing should not be glamorized as is done these days to market sex in 'first' world countries. A mother should be a good example to her daughter. Daughters should dress in such attire that would not disgrace or put shame on the family, whether she is being monitored or not. In the same spirit a man should not be effeminate in his dressing for whatever reason. It leads to perversion as it draws the attention of perverse men towards such dressers.

In many regions of the world, the weather dictates the mode of dressing to protect the body from the physical prevailing element, like heat or cold, wind or rain, snow, even dust. In very cold regions, pants are a common mode of dressing for both sexes, but there is a subtle difference between the cut, color, and accessories; also the top or blouse and the jacket are not the same. The difference can be clear if the mind of the wearer is clear.

Africans are very colorful and graceful in their native attire. It is also a mark of identification that anyone can be proud of. Men and women can make clothes of the same materials in different ways; women will be definitely recognized as different from men in their attire

.Unisex is not an option for a child of God; it is confusing apparel if you cannot distinguish a man from a woman.

We can enjoy many options in African styles and other people can copy these for their beauty and elegance. Imagine the beauty of Yoruba wedding attire that has been copied by many others. The colorful and charming Kente of the Ghanians is admirable and is now being used as college scarves in some American colleges. The wedding attire made of this material for a lady is smart and beautiful; and for a man it is noble.

The general West African Boubou is queenly and admirable especially when worn with the headgear. And what about the smartness and elegance of "Up and Down" generally worn by many Africans now? This could be worn to the office on casual days without drawing attention adversely. These African costumes and many others can be made of fabric materials such as Kente, Aso oke, Tie & Die, Cotton prints, brocade, satins, to mention a few, without breaking a bank.

Africans are renowned for their beautiful accessories like beads, leather bags and shoes for women, shoes and decorated staffs for the men. A man will be recognized as distinguished in his big Agbada for occasions like weddings or attending church on Sundays, Buba and Soro (trouser) are gorgeous for casual outings and the likes. These are clothing to be proud of and must continue to be of strong identification to avoid being lost in global anonymity

FOOD

The Bible reveals to us the power of nutrition as a way to prevent diseases, to sustain our strength and energy and to improve health and promote growth. In a sense, we are what we eat.

The Holy Spirit dwells in the body of a believer. For this reason, a believer should keep his body healthy and free from anything that can destroy it, things like pollutants, drugs, alcohol, overeating and even immorality. Both Scripture and common sense tell us to care for ourselves so that we can glorify God with our bodies.

In recent past, Africans ate a lot of fresh food, grains, vegetables, fruits, fish and meat. Many of them live to ripe old age of between eighty and a hundred years without the present day diseases like cancer, ulcer, diabetes, heart disease, arthritis, etc. Africans of the past had lovely nice smooth skin and healthy teeth. Overeating was a very rare occurrence and many of them lived healthy lifestyles with plenty of exercise at their daily jobs and evening entertainment like wrestling, dancing, games and tournaments.

Now, with 'civilization' at home and abroad, healthy foods have been replaced with processed food, sugary drinks, and snacks, with little or no vegetables in their diet. Africans are generally not fat people, but it is amazing to see how fat and unhealthy some African young adults have become in their countries of immigration. Fast food is their food of choice, and they top it up with sugar filled soda drinks. It is extremely easy to put on weight than to shed the weight.

Because of the strains and stresses of life in some cities, many people eat to console themselves without thinking of the consequences it will have on their health. The proverb 'when in Rome do as the Romans do', should not be adhered to when it concerns food and morals in first world countries.

In most cities of the world, there are shops that sell African foodstuffs. Other healthy food shops can be found if an effort is made to find them. There are restaurants too where you can pick healthy menus if the determination is to eat healthy. Food is good, but man must control what he eats and not allow food to take control of him.

Phillipians 3:19 warns people:
> *Whose end is destruction, whose God is*
> *their belly, and whose glory is their shame,*
> *who mind earthly thing.*

Proverbs 23: 1-3
> *When thou sittest to eat with a ruler,*
> *consider diligently what is before thee, and*
> *put a knife to thy throat, if thou be a*
> *Man given to appetite.*
> *Be not desirous of his dainties, for they*
> *are deceitful meat.*

This is not limited to rulers alone, but also tempting parties, restaurants and fast food cafes.

Proverbs 23: 20-21 specifies:

> *Be not among wine bibbers, among*
> *riotous eaters of flesh.*
> *For the drunkard and the gluttony shall*
> *come to poverty, and drowsiness shall*
> *clothe a man with rags.*

Proverbs 25:16 warns

> *Hast thou found honey? Eat as much*
> *as is sufficient for thee, lest thou be*
> *filled there with and vomit it.*

Some people assume they are sober because they cannot afford to keep the habit of drinking; these same people are unable to control themselves when it is offered freely. They are the types who will throw up after a few drinks because their body is not accustomed to it. Each immigrant should cautiously watch out in order not to embarrass himself or herself..

Ephesians 5:18 says

> *And be not drunk with wine, where in*
> *Is excess; but be filled with the Spirit.*

A life controlled by the Holy Spirit is superior to any alternative, including a life filled with chemicals or other addictive food or drink.

Felicia Oguntomilade

There are two references in the Bible about fat people and the pictures are not pretty.

Judges 3:17-22 told the story of King Eglon, the fat king of Moab and how he died.

The second was Eli in 1 Samuel 4:18. He was the high priest who had no control over his gluttonous overgrown kids. They all fed fat on the sacrifices offered to God by the people of Israel. He and the children died shamefully the same day because of their sin that originated in greed and disregard for God.

Fear, respect, love and reverence for God are the beginnings of wisdom. Healthy eating and drinking should be a common sense habit; and such a habit should be acquired to keep the temple of God holy. Africans should look back at the way our ancestors eat and do likewise. They should similarly nfluence others by their example and posture..

TALENTS

As a race Africans are very strong, agile and sporty. This can be observed in athletic performances at home and abroad. It is a national pastime exercise for adult and adolescents and even children to wrestle, play football, run, swim, jump, hunt, dance, sing and do physical farming. Because of the climate and the needs of each community, Africans grow tough and strong. It is not surprising to see them excel in such activities where there are facilities to develop their talents further. It will be advisable for talented young men and women to take opportunity of their new surroundings to develop further and influence others by being mentors for others who need such influence in their lives.

Sports happen to be lucrative in some countries. Immigrants should take the opportunity and be wise with their earnings, since there is a limit to the number of years such activities can generate income for an individual, before age takes its toll.

Africans are not just brawn without brain. In many rich countries of the world like America, England, Canada, Germany even Saudi Arabia, Africans can be found in all the major intellectual professions. Considering their home background with only bare opportunities, it is amazing to observe the excellence of Africans' performance in the country of their new abode. In the field of health, there are doctors, pharmacists, nurses, biochemists and laboratory technicians. In computer science, many Africans are acknowledged as masters of the technology.

In pure academics, they are professors in universities as well as in colleges all over the world. In the field of music and arts, Africans excel whenever they are exposed and opportune to show their talents. Music and arts seem to come naturally with Africans; these show further in the vitality and jollity of their festivals and ceremonies. In the spiritual field, Africans are ardent worshipers hence there are giants of Christian faith coming from Africa to bless other creatures of God in other parts of the world.

In ending this chapter on how African immigrants can influence others, this adage can be quoted:

"Charity begins at home."

In all our achievements, training, experiences, adjustments, and even the strains and stresses they go through; many Africans have benefited and matured beautifully; they in turn must endeavor to share all these with fellow Africans back at home and those less fortunate around us. African countries especially south of the Sahara are still very poor economically and equally politically immature.

A few dollars or pounds sent home to immediate families is always much appreciated. Small money goes a long way to meet the essential needs of those families and in the education of younger members of the family. Community needs too can be met in this wise. While helping economically, a little giving can be buttressed with sound economic advice to the people concerned. This act of giving reinforces our bonding with kin and kin at home; and it enhances their comfort and security while givers receive the joy and blessing of giving.

There are many Africans abroad who can safely influence the political development back home. They should do so with wisdom and discretion. They have relatives at home in positions of power who can benefit from sound advice

African Immigrants

from their own kith and kin who have seen politics practiced in relatively cleaner and more mature ways.

Prayer is a" number- one" help that countries back home in Africa will surely benefit from. It is a duty of every born -again, spirit –filled, Christo-centric and sanctified child of God, to intercede for their homeland for the sustenance of peace and good government.

1 Timothy 2:1-2 enjoins believer to heed:
I exhort therefore that, first of all,
supplications, prayers, intercessions and
giving of thanks be made for all men:
For the kings, and for all that are in authority:
that we may lead a quiet
and peaceable life in all godliness
and honesty.
For this is good and acceptable
in the sight of God our Savior.

Prayer can change or improve circumstances because it is asking for divine help, which surpasses all human power and authority. Today we can see what faith in God and prayer to God has done in the country of Uganda. It has changed and transformed the horrible, nightmarish, ghost-hunting government of yesteryears to a peaceful God-fearing government with peace assuredly settling on that nation.

The hand of God can be seen in many African countries where many believers have resorted to God alone when powerful cruel greedy rulers have milked their countries dry and oppressed their countrymen. God remains sovereign and still answers prayer. He is almighty and is no respecter of persons. With God around, there is no superman but there is a God who is superior to every man and to those demi- gods who will eventually give account to their creator.

Psalm 75: 5-9 warns

> *Lift not up your horn on high: speak*
> *Not with stiff neck.*
> *For promotion cometh neither from the East*
> *Nor from the West nor from the South.*
> *But God is the judge he putteth down*
> *one, and setteth up another.*

Queen Mary of England was quoted once that she feared the prayers of John Knox more than she feared all the armies of Scotland. She knew and felt what she was talking about - the power of prayer. Therefore, for believers to effect the desired change in their nations, they must utilize this potent and free weapon. Also, immigrants must also pray for the leaders of their 'new' countries of abode as directed by the Scripture. It is by God's grace that they are settled in those countries and therefore must live according to God's instruction so that they will continue to live a peaceable life. They will do well to live as good citizens and to reflect their faith there by being a good example to others.

PRAYER

Father God, I appreciate your love and your grace over me. I thank you for the opportunity you have given me to be where I am. I pray that all you have given me in talent and resources will be economically and beneficially used for your glory and for the benefit of those in need. I pray Lord that I will reflect you in my thought, word and deed and for your name to be glorified. Thank you Father for who you are. I pray this in Jesus Name. Amen.

7

SAVED TO SERVE

    Various African cultures accept that the lifetime is a journey to somewhere; hence many worship different gods and ancestors to seek their favor for now and for yonder. Indeed life is a pilgrimage. The Holy Bible teaches and informs readers to appreciate that there is more to life than the few decades spent on earth compared with life in eternity. Whether one is a believer or not does not stop the plan of the creator; that there is eternity to contend with. There are only two destinations for man's eternity. It is either in paradise that leads to the New city Jerusalem or in hell that finally terminates in the Lake of Fire burning inexhaustibly with brimstone. The picture of both is well described in the Scripture; and it is not a pretty picture in the Lake of fire at all, there is no fun there either.

Matthew 25:41

> *Then shall he say unto them on the left hand,*
> *Depart from me, ye cursed, into everlasting*
> *fire, prepared for the devil and his angels.*

Matthew 25:46

> *And these shall go away into everlasting*
> *punishment; but the righteous into life eternal.*

Revelation 20:13-15

> *And the sea gave up the dead, which were*
> *In it; and death and hell delivered up*
> *The dead, which were in them; and they*
> *Were judged every man according to his works.*
>
> *And death and hell were cast into the lake*
> *Of fire. This is the second death.*
> *And whatsoever was not found written*
> *In the book of Life was cast into the*
> *Lake of fire.*

Those in the lake of fire will be living in torment unimaginable forever. There will be no repentance or change of mind there.

Here on earth is the place to make up the mind where to spend eternity. The only way is through Jesus Christ who is the Way, the Truth, and the Life. Since nobody can absolutely determine well in advance when he will die, the sure bet is now;

procrastination can put a person in jeopardy of hell fire. Now, for believers in the Lord Jesus Christ who are already saved, and on this pilgrimage journey to life eternal with Christ, they are to occupy until He comes back. There are responsibilities of true discipleship that will earn believers favor of God with benefits in eternity, i.e. preparing for destination.

In life's journey, before traveling to another country, the traveler purchases the ticket, books a hotel for lodging, checks on prevailing conditions in the country of destination and prepares for a comfortable stay over there. It is similar with the journey to eternity for believers. Jesus Christ, who paid for it on the cross, because a sinner cannot afford it, has already purchased the ticket for a believer. Thank God! Jesus who said He was going to prepare a place(heavenly mansions)for his followers yonder has promised accommodation. What a grace. All that is left for every believing saint is to prepare to enjoy the benefits yonder by following His instructions given before He ascended to heaven.

While He was physically on earth, Jesus was busy doing his Father's will. He healed the sick, raised the dead, fed the hungry, cast out demons, performed numerous miracles, revealed His Father to his disciples, taught His disciples and all those who came to Him, cleansed the Temple and so many other good things. He encouraged the disciples that they would do greater works than He had done in His Name and by His power. In Matthew 25: 13-20, He commissioned the disciples when He was about to ascend to heaven:

And Jesus came and spake unto them saying,
All power is given unto me in heaven and earth.
Go ye therefore, and teach all nations,
baptizing them in the name of the Father,
and of the Son, and of the Holy Ghost.
Teaching them to observe all things
whatsoever I have commanded you: and
lo, I am with you always, even unto
the end of the world. Amen.

This is a divine instruction backed up by divine power to all followers of the Lord Jesus Christ; an enablement entrusted to all who are faithful to follow in His footsteps as long as they live.

Someone may be challenging this call to ask whether all believers should become pastors, Bible teachers, preachers, evangelists and such other theological professions .. Yea, all are called to be in the service of the Lord, wherever they may be, or whatever profession they may be in. Luke was a doctor, Paul was a tent maker, Lydia was a clothes dyer, Dorcas was a seamstress, David was a shepherd boy; even the Samaritan woman who met Jesus at the well of Jacob had no known business other than being a loose woman periodically changing husbands; yet she became the first evangelist in her town heralding that Jesus, the Messiah had indeed come. Abraham who became a pillar of faith and a friend of God remained a herdsman. In whatever vocation or occupation a believer may be in, he or she can be gracefully used to answer the call of God to his service. Another person can be influenced for Christ in the way one practices one's daily occupation; such a person can become the gospel that people can read.

Christ can be seen in believers' talk, walk, and work and in relationship with others. A housewife too can be of great use. In her role, she can bring up her children to love God; and those children can become useful tools in the hands of God. Samuel's mother Hannah, Timothy's mother Eunice, Timothy's grandmother Lois: these were examples of godly mothers who influenced their children to be great servants of the Lord; they were of such importance to the Lord that their names and their deeds were recorded in the Holy Bible, the Oracle of God.

A slave girl also was used to introduce her master a leprous captain Naman to the prophet of the Lord and he was healed of leprosy. God can use anybody for his glory. The loving young widow Ruth, who had faith in the God of Israel and showed so much humility and loyalty to her mother-in-law, was used by the Lord to become the grandmother of David, king of Israel. David is a great lover of God. There are endless ways that God can use available vessels to win souls and achieve great things for the entrenchment of His Kingdom . Believers are all kings and priests and ambassadors of God Almighty, the King of Kings.

African Immigrants

John Newton, a ruthless slave merchant was convicted by the Holy Spirit and was used mightily by God. He was later appointed to preach the faith he had worked so hard to destroy.

He was the writer of the famous song: "Amazing Grace"

- *Amazing grace! How sweet the sound*
That saved a wretch like me!
I once was lost but now am found,
Was blind but now I see
- *'Twas grace that taught my heart to fear,*
And grace my fears relieved;
How precious did that grace appear
The hour I first believed!
- *The Lord has promised good to me,*
His word my hope secures;
He will my shield and portion be
As long as life endures.
- *Through many dangers, toils and snares*
I have already come;
'Tis grace hath brought me safe thus far;
And grace will lead me home.
- *When we've been here ten thousand years,*
Bright shining as the sun,
We've no less days to sing God's praise
Than when we'd first begun.

Felicia Oguntomilade

John Newton 1725 - 1807

Stanza 5 by John P. Rees 1828 - 1900

Most human beings labor and strive in this world for various secular reasons: to earn a living and maintain a family, to have reasonable shelter, to protect self and loved ones, and to earn prestige among colleagues.

Some even get more ambitious and labor to conquer countries and races and to be head of empires. Some people want to be rich and possibly be the richest. All these goals may be attained legally or illegally. The means have its consequences because the end does not always justify the means. Many people reap what they sow here on earth and they pass some consequences to the generation after them. Whatever any man may achieve in this world; when he dies without Christ, it is a gloomy eternity.

Nobody carries any material earthly possession with him to eternity, for it will be no use there. When a believer dies, all that he has done for Christ will have been saved up or accumulated for eternity where he will receive the benefit with interest. A definite reward is promised for people who are faithful in the use of the talents entrusted to them. This is revealed in Matthew 20: 1-16 in the parable of the laborers. Christians are all laborers in God's vineyard. Christians are called to be light to the world, to be soul winners and to be salt to the world.

Daniel 12:3 declares:

> *And they that be wise shall shine as*
> *the brightness of the firmament; and they*
> *that turn many to righteousness as*
> *the stars forever and ever.*

Those believers, who live in this world of darkness, must pass on the torch of the truth of the Gospel so that unbelievers around them may see the light and quit darkness. Christians should do this, and the Holy Spirit will do the convicting of the souls, and many of these souls will yield to Christ.

It is not always easy to win souls; it did not come easy for Christ our mentor. Perseverance and love for souls should motivate believers to follow in Christ's footsteps. There is the risk of being mocked; and there may be suffering and other trials encountered in seeking the salvation of souls.

2 Timothy 2:12 emphasizes:

> *If we suffer, we shall also reign with*
> *Him, if we deny Him, He also will*
> *deny us.*

By winning souls for Christ there is Crown of Rejoicing.

James 1:12

> *Blessed is the man that endureth temptation:*
> *for when he is tried he shall receive the*

> *Crown of Life, which the Lord has promised*
> *to them that love him*

Similarly 2 Corinthians 5:10 confirms
> *For we must all appear before the*
> *judgement seat of Christ; that everyone*
> *may receive the things done in his*
> *body, according to that he hath done,*
> *whether be it good or bad.*

There is also a **Crown of Life** for tried and triumphant saints who are loyal unto death. This is the Martyr's crown in Rev. 2:10

1 Peter 5: 2-4 reveals the award **of Crown of Glory** thus:
> *Feed the flock of God which is among you,*
> *Taking the oversight thereof, not by constraint,*
> *But willingly; not for filthy lucre, but of a ready mind.*
> *Neither as being lords over God's heritage,*
> *But being examples to the flock. And when*
> *The Chief Shepherd shall appear,*
> *Ye shall receive a Crown of Glory,*
> *That fadeth not away.*

This is the Crown for faithful pastors and priests.

There is also a **Crown of Righteousness,** which is for loving His appearance by living in the light of that blessed hope.

1 Corinthians 9:25 reveals how to win an Overcomer's Crown. This is an **incorruptible crown** for victorious living. It is for believers who are spiritual in living a life of temperance and self-control. They walk in the spirit

Whilst all the above-named crowns will be shared after Rapture at the **Bema seat of Christ,** there are also many other enduring rewards here on earth for being in Christ and doing his will. Chief of these rewards are:

(a) Peace of mind
(b) Rejoicing in spirit
(c) Strength and power of the enabling Holy Spirit for the work
(d) Fulfilling and purposeful living
(e) Hope for eternal life.

These rewards are priceless, amazing and cannot be obtained by any other means except through Jesus.

While a believer is working faithfully, humbly and with love, he experiences this spiritual growth. Every barrier crossed through Christ draws the believer nearer in his relationship to the Lord. Being a beneficiary of divine love, privilege and power makes the believer more humble and more dependent on the source of His life and strength.

Christ Himself said in John 15:5:
I am the vine; ye are the branches;

> *He that abideth in me, and I in him, the same bringeth forth much fruits; for without me ye can do nothing.*

God must be acknowledged all times in a believer's work. All glory belongs to God. He will not share his glory with any man. So men beware!

Phillipians 4:13:
> *We can do all things through Christ that strengthens us.*

In conclusion of this book, readers should recognize the sovereignty and trascendence of God over all His creation, and yet His functioning ability ie his immanence within his creation. He is present everywhere and there is no other God.

God cares and loves mankind. He is aware of everybody's situation and is ready to back up those who put their trust in Him and surrender to his Lordship.

The earth is the Lord's and all that dwell therein, the compass of the world and they that dwell therein; and God can make his grace abound. He abhors laziness. He honors hard honest work. He does not object to honest riches but he hates the love of money that is the root of evil. He blesses believers so that they can be a blessing to other people. The more a believer is drawn to Christ, the more he is drawn out of a perplexed rat race of this unfruitful worldliness to a peaceful life in God's kingdom. A believer has that peace that passes all understanding; for indeed the believer appreciates that God is able to supply all his needs according to his riches in glory by Christ Jesus.

There are a couple of age-long questions that many unbelievers have frantically sought answers for; , despite all available resources, science and technology, there has been no suitable answers. It is only when an unbeliever comes to Christ that he gets a solution to some personal unanswered problems in his life.

"What is the purpose of life and what happens after death?"

Thank God, a believer, a born again Christian knows who he is, why he is on earth. He knows what he is doing and for what purpose he is doing it. The believer knows where he is going after death; in fact, he knows already that a mansion is already prepared for him. The believer knows in whom he trusts and he feels secure in the Lord. The believer knows that Christ in him is the hope of glory. The believer is not perfect but he is working at it with the help of the Holy Spirit.

What a prospect!

What a hope!

What a life.

The believer will not want to change this way for any other way. It is great to be a child of God, a joint heir with Christ, a member of the royal family of the King of Kings.

To God alone be the glory forever. Amen.

CONCLUDING PRAYER

My Father and my God, I give glory to you for who you are.

I adore and worship you, for you are worthy of all the praise and honor I can ever give to you.

I thank you for what you have made of me and the hope I have in you.

I thank you for your promises to me according to your word.

I pray for the enablement to live according to your purpose because I know it is the best for me.

I am willing to be directed by you, Lord.

Lead me and I will follow;.

I am available Lord, use me for your glory and make me a blessing to others.

I need your favor in all my undertakings and let your light shine through me and radiate that light to wherever I may go so that I can be light to my world.

In Jesus Name I pray. Amen.

CONCLUSION

It is sufficiently recognized that most immigrants have genuine reasons to leave their homeland for foreign land; It could be for the pursuit of educational goals; it could be for job opportunities that are abundant overseas. Others have migrated to seek asylum because of persecution or injustice.in their homeland; Many have followed their spouses into foreign land. Some too could have escaped into foreign lands to enjoy their loots, while many have been lucky to win the coveted 'Diversity immigrants (Lottery) visa' –good for them. There are also survivors of old immigrants who were immigrants not by choice but by force of evil trade called 'slavery'.

Indeed, God knows why one sojourns overseas; to Him, it is not by accident, it is part of His purposeful or permissive will within His eternal purpose.

Readers should be reminded that both social and religious life will be much different from what immigrants are used to in their homeland and should not be despondent, but look up to the Creator of mankind who is omniscient, omnipotent and omnipresent, and He who loves His creatures so much that He desired the best for them if they surrender to Him and acknowledge Him for who He is. He is sovereign over all nations.

Immigrants should be ready to make necessary adjustments to live peaceably and obey the laws of the land of the new abode, because the rulers are all God's agents for His purpose. Immigrants are encouraged to be positive and proactive; They should be able to influence others positively in Godly virtues: in family life, in showing respect to elders, in dressing modestly, in healthy living, in making the best use of their talents at work and at play in honesty and integrity, and remembering to show love to people around them in their foreign lands and extend generosity appropriately to those people left back home.

Finally, immigrants should know the Lord Jesus Christ and therefore completely submit to Him in all their ways.

May the Lord bless all my readers and make them shining lights in our dark world !

BIBLIOGRAPHY
African immigrants: Living a Godly life

1. All biblical references are taken from King James Version of the Holy Bible (KJV)

2. Barros, Manuel: Y A P 1986, A I b.

3. Caceras, Elena: Fifty years In America through the Back door

4. Daniels, Roger: Coming to America © by Visual Education Corporation

5. Graham, Billy: Unto The Hills—A Daily Devotional Book © Word Publishing, Dallas

6. Graham, Billy: Crusade Speech Ibid

7. Newton, John: Book of Hymns by Tyndale House Publishers

8. Rahenville, Leonard: Treasury of Prayer

9. Scriven, Joseph M: One Yearbook of Hymns by Tyndale House publishers Inc.

10. Whittier, John G.: Songs of Praise

Printed in the United States
23216LVS00006B/1-90